A Law Unto Themselves: The Media and the Criminal Justice System

Mary Ann Farkas

and

Frank Burke

Published by
CreateSpace Independent Publishing Platform
North Charleston, South Carolina

ISBN: 1511781165
ISBN-13: 978-1511781169

Library of Congress Catalog Card Number: 2015906592

Contents

i

ACKNOWLEDGMENTS

As authors of any volume as heavily involved with history as this, we have become aware that sources may well be too numerous to mention and acknowledgments too excessive to list. Among those who have contributed significantly to our work, we first wish to thank Dr. Armand Thieblot, who not only clarified the direction of our efforts but was extremely generous with his time and advice in reviewing in advance multiple drafts of the manuscript. His encouragement of this effort, when it was most needed, is invaluable. Mr. James T. Bennett likewise "lighted our path" in a solid direction and with valuable advice. Mr. John Maclay and Attorney James Harding gave multiple helpful suggestions and views from an experienced and educated perspective. Dr. Ronald Rubin, who read many of the chapters by Dr. Mary Ann Farkas, contributed very interesting and thoughtful feedback. Beth Fedyn's informed judgment led us to open the subject to a wider audience.

The staff at the Marquette University library was incredibly responsive and helpful in locating relevant materials in their collections, as well as securing others from outside. Likewise, the students in Dr. Farkas's classes who inspired the original idea and later advanced worthwhile critiques in a number of areas also contributed.

Deb Tyszka provided a selection of excellent cover designs. Jeff Farkas was always ready to run to the library and to search out needed documentation.

This book would have impossible without the persistent, perseverance, intellect, and skills of Peggy Towner Burke. A volume that is composed of multiple independent instances requires tremendous organizational skills, and from the start, she maintained the integrity of purpose and added markedly to the quality of the content. No task was too big for her, and her typing, proofreading, and correspondence with publishers and other involved individuals left the authors free to concentrate on the main points.

Insofar as this volume is an attempt to better the public understanding of its subject and to seek improvement from both sides and in their mutual relationship, it is hoped that it will contribute in some way to the civic and social betterment of a world that will belong to our children and grandchildren. Our love for them and their future is a large part of our motivation.

PREFACE

The need for this book first became apparent in a course on Criminal Justice taught by Dr. Mary Ann Farkas at Marquette University. In an effort to vividly illustrate the interplay between the media and the justice system, Dr. Farkas and Mr. Frank Burke prepared a segment citing some of the most significant media-influenced cases of the 20th century. In a class numbering 27 students, of whom the majority were studying law, none were familiar with the Leopold Loeb case; only three had heard of the Lindbergh kidnapping; and just nine correctly identified Jeffrey Dahmer—even though his crimes occurred within a 10-block radius of their classroom. When presented with the facts and details, however, all were curious to learn more.

In contemplating a tool that would fulfill both an educational need and increase public awareness of the critical web whose strands join the courts, the police, the media, and the public with the defendant at the center, the authors quickly realized the importance of context.

Today many, if not most, school systems have abandoned the traditional teaching of history in a chronological framework. Historical and political subjects are dealt with in an isolated fashion. Lacking an appreciation of what came before and affected the subsequent events results in an inability to appreciate their full significance. This is especially true when dealing with the news media—which is itself a creature of the moment. To correct this defect, the authors have selected cases relevant to the development of the media/justice relationship and have prefaced each one with a brief description of "The Time and the Place."

As the concept of the "media" has evolved from the traditional newspaper to the Internet and social media, it has effected change at all levels. More people are involved, in some aspect or other, than ever before. With more eyes on the system, dubious "proofs" in the form of documents and even videos are more quickly and easily refuted. On the other hand, as recent cases have shown, a media frenzy can and has caused the public to prejudge cases early on. In its ability to marshal adherents and mobs and to be seized upon by officials and others for political purposes, it cannot only subvert the system but let loose monsters in the street.

It is the hope of the authors that a greater knowledge of the process and how it evolved will enable all concerned—the justice system, the media and the public—to learn from the past and approach the future with appropriate restraint.

Chapter 1
Setting the Narrative—An Introduction

Throughout history, among virtually all peoples, a fascination with crime—especially violent crime and sex crime—is present. The story of Cain and Abel occurs in the first book of the Bible and is followed by many more tales of crime and punishment, both earthly and divine. In early times, and even now in more primitive societies, public punishments ranging from the stocks to floggings to executions were viewed as a means of deterring potential criminals from acting on their impulses. Regardless of a body of evidence to the contrary, deterrence is often cited as the primary reason in favor of capital punishment.

Despite the somber message intended, punishments, especially executions, were replete with crowds of onlookers who turned the ghastly displays to celebrations. For those who could not attend, or who sought a deeper understanding of the circumstances surrounding the crime being punished, the media—in its many forms—has capitalized on this fascination. From the earliest ballads recounting bloody doings to the 17th and 18th century pamphlets narrating the careers of executed criminals to today's movies and electronic media, the fascination remains.

Psychologically, there are various reasons for this continuing morbid fascination, some of which overlap. The idea that "crime does not pay" appeals to our sense of self-righteousness and the congratulatory belief that we are better than the criminal. Others are fascinated with the mechanism of justice, as evidenced in both police procedures and the legal system and illustrated in numerous stories, books, movies, and TV programs, some of which have impacted aspects of the system they portray. (A prime example of this is the so-called "CSI effect" that, among other things, has served to prejudice jurors in favor of sometimes questionable DNA evidence and to presume even the smallest scrap of evidence can be definitively analyzed.) Another viewpoint identifies with the criminal and wonders what it would be like to live experiences so different from one's own. Whatever their motivations, the vast majority of observers bear one thing in common: they watch from a safe distance, feeling—except in imagination—neither the agony of crime victims nor the punishment of the perpetrators. Insulated from the reality, their information has been sifted to maximize their vicarious pleasure.

For a certain number of individuals and their families, however, a combination of circumstances can thrust them into a situation in which what might once have been viewed as a news item becomes an all-too-grim reality. They experience firsthand the nexus of procedure, ambition, publicity, and fate that occurs when the justice system and the media cross.

Consider the following true examples:

- You and your family have managed a small but successful daycare center for many years. It has an extremely good name, and a number of the children once cared for keep in touch with you well into their adulthood. Without warning, you are arrested and charged with molesting several of the children in your care. As accusations mount, your picture and name are all over the local newspapers and on TV. Supposedly, in private sessions with a psychologist, some children say that they were molested in a magic room or by a Bad Clown. Others claim that you sexually penetrated them with knives and that they were tied, naked, to trees outside your building in full view of a major highway. You cannot believe that such far-fetched accusations can stand up to scrutiny, but prosecutors introduce an expert witness who claims that the accusations reflect actual psychological trauma and that you are indeed guilty. You, and other family members are convicted and sent to prison. As time passes, the hysteria dies down. Despite multiple proofs of your innocence, an ambitious District Attorney presses the Governor to refuse to grant you clemency as proof that she is "tough on crime." When you are finally let go, your life has been shattered, your resources drained, and your reputation, in the eyes of many, ruined.

• For no apparent reason, your computer has slowed down and is not responsive to certain functions, so you take it to a store that does repairs and leave it with them. Two days later, police are at your door. You are arrested and charged with possessing thousands of pictures of child pornography. You're informed that they have been found on your hard drive, and there is no other way they could have gotten there except that you downloaded them. The computer is confiscated as evidence, and you are identified in the local newspaper and on TV and radio. You are forbidden to associate with any young children, and you are shunned by neighbors and former friends. Even family members begin to doubt your word. Working with your lawyer, you hire several experts who, over time and through painstaking analysis and experimentation, prove that the images on your computer originated in Asia and were "parked" there without your knowledge. You are acquitted, but the cost of your defense has consumed all of your savings, your reputation has been seriously damaged, and there are those who will forever doubt your innocence.

In either of these cases, and in other instances in which innocent people have found themselves facing the combined machinery of the justice system and the media, victims have asked the pointed question, "Why is this happening to me?" A more pertinent, if less emotional, question might be, "Who or what set the narrative that assumes such a definite presumption of guilt?"

Setting the Narrative

Criminal cases rarely emerge with all the facts present and in order. In the early stages of any investigation, the police and other investigative authorities examine clues, identify evidence, question individuals, and seek to piece together a coherent description that defines the guilty party or parties and will hold up in court. Once they are satisfied that they have identified the perpetrator(s), the focus moves from identifying other possible subjects or circumstances to building a case in support of their conclusion. The prosecuting authorities then review the component pieces to ensure that they fit within the bounds of whatever charges they seek to bring and develop the presentation that they will make at trial.

Crafting the narrative to fit the evidence, however, is not foolproof. Especially when it comes to high-profile cases, the police are under heavy pressure to present a solution in the shortest possible time. Further, the successful prosecution of cases is a major factor in advancing the careers of both police officers and prosecutors. Some can, and do, succumb to the temptation to bend the evidence through selective emphasis, by distorting the facts, or in extreme cases, by withholding exculpatory information from the defense. The late British journalist, Ludovic Kennedy, in his book on the Lindbergh case, *The Airman and the Carpenter*, quoted the crime writer and historian, Julian Symmons, who said:

> At a trial, events are often seen in a distorted perspective. A violent event has taken place, and we work backwards from it, considering primarily the evidence bearing on that event. If we work forwards in a natural sequence, from a natural starting point, the evidence may wear a very different appearance.

As far as the public is concerned, the media is the sole or major source of information about crime and the justice system since they are not likely to experience crime or to be involved with the system, but the fact is that the reporting of crime in the media is not a value-neutral activity. News production reflects the ideology of news executives, editors, and other workers. This can manifest itself in a variety of ways. Research demonstrates that employees of major news organizations, especially in large cities, overwhelmingly lean toward the political Left. The liberal ideological bias can become evident in cases in which the perpetrator's economic, racial, and/or social strata is cited as a factor for his actions or as a reason to mitigate his deeds. The increasing prevalence of so-called "hate crimes" legislation has resulted in a tendency to sensationalize cases that fall into that category—especially when the victim is a member of a minority group. Clearly, information presented by the media is not unimpeachable or irreproachable but rather may reflect the ideology, philosophy, or political orientation of the communicator.

Further, the relationship between the media and its audience is not one-sided, as media authorities would have us believe. The audience's role is viewed as more interpretive. Certainly, as the public grows savvier in the use of the new electronic media, they have the capacity to weigh and check sources of the news information. Whether or not they will use that capability wisely is another matter.

On a day-to-day basis, there is an almost limitless supply of crimes, especially in large urban areas, available for media coverage. The media and the criminal justice system have an overall cooperative, mutually beneficial relationship. Each has a similar need to accomplish its objectives, and in practice, can even serve the other's interests. The media relies on criminal justice officials as sources of information on the crime and its criminal processing. The justice officials often rely on the media for other purposes. For example, law enforcement officials may use the media to circulate a sketch of an alleged perpetrator, or a judge or district attorney running for office may seek press coverage of a sensational case to garner public support.

Another instance in which the media imposes itself on the justice system involves political figures. National politicians may choose a particular crime "problem" which they believe will resonate with the public. President Richard Nixon advocated for heightened drug enforcement and called for a "war on drugs." Candidates for local offices frequently like to portray themselves as "tough on crime." Where they are connected, through friendship or otherwise, with the media, their exploits can be over-reported, or stories regarding cases they are currently working on can be described with a decided slant that benefits the prosecution.

The phenomenon of criminals contacting the media or figures in the media directly can have the effect of creating a mutual bond between the two. Intent on the part of the criminal can include personal publicity, the ability to taunt the police or other perceived adversaries, the search for sympathy, a forum to publicize a political position or declaration, or any number of other rational or irrational reasons. Serial murderer Dennis Rader demanded media attention, writing, "How many do I have to kill before I get my name in the paper or some national attention?"

Criminals can also manipulate the media by intentionally turning a media event, such as a televised trial, into a media circus. Serial killer Ted Bundy is a notorious example. In his televised trials, Bundy was the "consummate gamesman," acting as his own defense attorney. He relished the attention and artfully played to his captive audience. During his time on death row, Bundy took great pleasure in granting lengthy interviews with the press.

On the part of the media, such a relationship can result in exclusivity, leverage with the police or prosecution for present or future favors, and journalistic prizes or awards. For the individual reporter, advantages include enhanced fame, the increased likelihood of being contacted in other situations, or opportunities on the lecture circuit and talk shows and even book deals (Jimmy Breslin, for example, would later write a fictionalized account of the Son of Sam killings in a novel entitled, ".44" (Viking Press, 1978, with Dick Schaap).

Due to relatively rapid technological advances, the term "media" is in a constant state of expansion and flux. It has virtually supplanted the word "press" which was a generic reference to printed newspapers and periodicals (and is referenced in the First Amendment to the United States Constitution). The scope of the change has not only revolutionized reportage but calls into question many of the traditions associated with journalism. In the past, access to sites ranging from crime scenes to presidential press (that word again) conferences has been granted through the use of a card or other credential identifying the bearer as the representative of an approved newsgathering organization.

Now, thanks to the electronic media, anyone who takes the time and trouble to set up a blog or to affiliate with a blog site can be styled a journalist.

As we move from the national scene through various communities and locations, we encounter wide differences in terms of values, preferences, and ideologies whose understandings are shaped by individual experiences and interactions with families, and spiritual and educational institutions. These translate in turn to the legal and justice system in ways ranging from acceptance or rejection of the death penalty, through laws governing firearm ownership to such seeming trivialities as traffic regulations.

No justice system is perfect, and instances are regularly discovered, by science or otherwise, in which the innocent have been found guilty or the guilty go free. In some of these cases, the media has played a complicit role.

The authors hope that the information presented here on the history and interaction of the media, the public, and other involved parties in the criminal justice system will promote a greater degree of awareness and a more analytical and active approach to one of the cornerstones of our personal freedom and safety. As the media continues to evolve and speeds the flow of information (both correct and incorrect), it is imperative that the public be more active and skeptical consumers by analyzing and reflecting upon the information made available, rather than simply accepting a narrative that may or may not be accurate.

Part I
The Birth of Media Sensationalism

Introduction

For the media to come of age as a force capable of impacting the criminal justice system, several factors must converge. These include: an audience capable of providing media support; an infrastructure able to report, process, and distribute the information; and a justice system susceptible to public and media influence. In 1836, all these were present in New York City. The spark that was to ignite their interaction was the murder of a young prostitute named Helen Jewett.

Even more than the bizarre circumstances of her death and the subsequent trial and acquittal of her murderer, the case caught the imagination of the public in its exposition of the underworld of prostitution and the lives of both the prostitutes and their patrons. The case continues to fascinate and even in recent times has been the subject of investigative works, novels, and historic references.

Six years after the Jewett case, the mysterious death of Mary Cecilia Rogers—known to the public as "The Beautiful Cigar Girl"—elicited a similar flurry of press attention. Following the girl's disappearance, the discovery of her body—and later of additional pieces of "evidence," coupled with a cast of bizarre characters—turned the case into a combination mystery story and soap opera. Ironically, it would serve as the basis for the first fictionalized detective story based on an actual case.

While the Jewett and Rogers cases attracted media notoriety largely because of the peculiar circumstances surrounding them, the murder of architect Stanford White is a landmark event, not just in the details relating to the crime itself but in its revelations regarding the sordid details of the rich and socially prominent. In so doing, it drew aside the Victorian curtain of prudery and respectability and established itself as the first of many "crimes—and trials—of the century."

The Lindbergh case would become especially notable, not only for the horror of the crime—the kidnap and murder of a child—and the celebrity of his parents, but for the then-novel radio coverage that enabled millions to follow the trial in "real time." Replete with peripheral frauds and scandals, the case provided an ongoing radio drama for a Depression-weary public.

Even today, the Lindbergh case appears regularly in the media, and debate continues as to whether the inconclusive nature of the evidence, the police procedures, and the legal questions involved might have resulted in the execution of an innocent man.

Chapter 2
Setting Precedents—the Early Cases

Helen Jewett—The Time and the Place

In the early 19th century, the media consisted primarily of newspapers, pamphlets, and books. As a result of the Industrial Revolution, the printing industry had been revolutionized by steam-powered presses that not only increased output but also kept prices low. A wide variety of papers and periodicals catered to virtually every taste and need, ranging from the so-called "Penny Dreadfuls" featuring sensationalistic crime reporting to legitimate newspapers to business-related organs to the foreign language presses serving immigrant groups. A peculiar subset included a number of papers targeted to various social strata reporting largely on fashions, tastes, and entertainment.

As the primary port city with a population of 270,000, New York was not only rapidly growing but boasted a large population of transients including immigrants bound for the American interior, as well as merchant sailors, cattle drovers, business people and other visitors. As the city rapidly moved northward from the southern tip of Manhattan island, many of the older neighborhoods, especially around the so-called Five Points area, became overpopulated slums inhabited by immigrants. Crime and vice were rampant, as was public and gang violence.

Urban growth had likewise outstripped the demand for social services. The City would not have an organized police department until 1845. Until then, it was served and protected by various watchmen, marshals, constables, and local police. Often sponsored by politicians, volunteer firefighters were known to engage in fistfights over "turfs" while buildings burned. Firefighting techniques were primitive, and many of the older structures especially were highly flammable. On the evening of December 16th to December 17th, 1835, the "Great Fire of New York" destroyed between 500 and 700 buildings in lower Manhattan.

Prostitution extended through virtually all groups, ranging from the common streetwalkers who plied their trade in the dives and so-called "cribs" to the "girls of the town" living in richly decorated houses, entertaining leading social and political figures, attending numerous society balls, and indulging in elaborate pseudo-courtships. Helen Jewett was one of the latter.

The Helen Jewett Case

Born into a poor family in the vicinity in Augusta, Maine, Dorcas Doyen (her real name) was taken into the family of Judge Nathan Weston and sent to school. When sexual relationships with two local individuals compromised her reputation, she left town. In New York, her beauty, refined manners, and intelligence enabled her to secure positions in a sequence of upscale houses of prostitution. Along the way, she assumed several aliases, ultimately reinventing herself as Helen Jewett. At the time of her death, she resided in the house of Rosina Townsend at 41 Thomas Street.

New York in 1836 held a tolerant view of prostitution. Technically speaking, it was not against the law, although one could be prosecuted on complaint of running a disorderly house. Upper-class prostitutes frequented the theaters along the Bowery, and in some cases whole balconies were informally reserved for them and their patrons. Despite the efforts of reformers, religious figures, and others, the public and the police were accepting of the situation for a number of reasons, including a popular belief in the base nature of men and their inability to control their desires and impulses. Young men who came to the city to seek their fortunes were often single for an extended period—one that coincided with their sexual prime. This in turn created a mentality that in some quarters not only tolerated promiscuity but encouraged it. The fashionable young adherents to this lifestyle were referred to as "sporting men" and were numerous enough to support a series of newspapers and magazines with names such as the *Rake*, the *Whip*, and the *Libertine*. Such periodicals were typically filled with justification of—and support for— prostitution and its patrons.

One of the sporting men whose path crossed Helen's was the son of a Connecticut farmer and landowner named Richard Robinson. Like many of his contemporaries, Robinson had secured a position as clerk in a store, so as to learn the basics of business. In the custom of the time, he was introduced to Helen by another of her lovers/patrons, something that was considered a compliment to the woman. As was likewise customary, he used a brothel alias: Frank Rivers.

Typically, these young men pledged their loyalty to the woman even as they knew that she was entertaining any number of their associates and others. In addition to any regular agreed-on payment, the man was expected to bring her gifts such as jewelry or books. While sex was the causative factor, there was a companionate quality to such relationships. In the case of Helen Jewett and Richard Robinson, two people, both using created identities, engaged in a pantomime courtship that lasted some 10 months.

Sometime between 9:00 and 9:30 on the evening of Saturday, April 9th, 1836, Rosina Townsend opened the door to the man she knew as Frank Rivers. Helen had told her to expect him, and Rosina showed him to the back parlor where Helen met him. At about 11:00 p.m., Helen emerged and asked Rosina to bring up a bottle of champagne. When she delivered it, Rosina noticed Frank Rivers lying on the bed reading by candlelight.

At 3:00 a.m., another patron arrived at the house. Rosina Townsend, in answering the door, noticed a lamp that could have only belonged to Helen Jewett or to another "resident," Maria Stevens. Finding Stevens's room locked, she opened the door to Helen's room and was greeted with a cloud of smoke. After screaming for the night watchman, she returned and discovered Helen, her bloody head badly smashed and her body partially in flames. After extinguishing the fire, she examined the room and discovered that very little of the champagne had been consumed. In the back behind the house, she found a hatchet and Frank Rivers' cloak. A piece of string around the hatchet corresponded to a cord tied inside the cloak that enabled Robinson to carry it without detection. Clearly, this was murder and premeditated at that.

As word of the brutal murder spread, a throng of watchmen, police, the curious, and reporters descended on the Thomas Street brothel. Among them was the Scottish-born owner of the New York *Herald*, James Gordon Bennett. Ambitious, egotistical, and highly eccentric, Bennett sensed in the Jewett murder a story that could drive circulation. While most other papers confined the criminal news to the inside pages, Bennett promoted it as the primary story. The *Herald*, the *Sun*, and the *Transcript*, all penny newspapers, hastily sought about assembling (with varying degrees of accuracy) background stories on the victim. The major daily newspapers, which sold for 6 cents at the time, were primarily concerned with commercial, political, and financial news. Their coverage of crime was reflected in reports of the Police Court and the Court of General Sessions. As the Jewett case grew in notoriety, however, they were forced to increase their crime coverage.

With little doubt as to the identity of the perpetrator, Robinson was quickly indicted. His employer, Joseph Hoxie, hired a prominent attorney, and the presiding judge, Ogden Edwards, was both politically and socially well connected. In the weeks leading up to the trial, press coverage intensified. Enterprising print makers created images of Helen as she appeared in life—and death. The most sensational showed her body lying on the bed, nearly naked.

Despite the weight of circumstantial evidence against him, Robinson proclaimed his innocence. Bennett instinctively realized that by championing Robinson's cause, he could not only generate sales among the "sporting men" set but create further controversy that would help build the *Herald*'s readership. His intuition proved correct and, by mid-April, the three major penny newspapers topped 50,000 in circulation.

Excitement about the case was further fueled when a police clerk inadvertently released the diary found in Robinson's room. Containing a combination of adolescent ramblings, sexual and other observations, and descriptions of episodes of depression, the diary was excerpted in newspapers and published as a pamphlet.

After a lengthy trial characterized by contradictory testimony and highly slanted instructions from the judge, the jury took only 15 to 18 minutes to find Robinson not guilty. Subsequently, he departed for Texas, where he married and attained a measure of prosperity. Twenty years later, on a visit to Louisville, he took sick and died.

The story was over, but the effect of the Jewett case on the media, and vice versa, was a watershed for several reasons. In popularizing the penny press, it established what is today called tabloid journalism. In its microscopic (if not always correct) examination of the lives of Helen Jewett and Richard Robinson, it offered the public a voyeuristic glimpse into two vastly different, but overlapping, lifestyles: that of the socially prominent prostitute and, perhaps more significant, that of the many young clerks who came to the city to seek their fortunes, using the services of prostitutes in the process.

The Jewett case and its media mania provided material that would be used by moral reformers to back their contention that young girls like Helen, once in the big city, could easily become trapped in a web of seduction and immorality into which they in turn would lure innocent farm boys to their moral doom. Public acceptance of such reasoning would impact the justice system by creating a mindset that would ultimately outlaw prostitution and drive it underground. It would also contribute to the bias against "fallen" and "loose" women. In "pushing the envelope" of sensationalism, it was picked up by out-of-town papers (albeit with some delay) and became much more than a local event.

Justice was denied Helen Jewett. Despite the public tolerance that condoned her and her sisters in the sex trade, when it came to the legal system, there would always be distrust. Regardless of the weight of evidence, the testimony of the madam, Rosina Townsend, and her staff were, in the instructions of Judge Edwards, "without other testimony . . . not to be received." Then, as now, a popular media capable of conferring celebrity status on an individual like Richard Robinson could be complicit in establishing a narrative that bent public opinion and freed a murderer.

Mary Cecilia Rogers—The Time and the Place

Throughout the United States, the years between the Helen Jewett murder and the strange case of Mary Cecilia Rogers were marked by explosive growth. Inspired by the success of New York's Erie Canal (opened in 1825) and the prosperity that accrued to towns and cities along the new railway routes, the country embarked on a flurry of speculation that outran the capacity of the banking system, resulting in the Panic of 1837. But, it was only a temporary setback. Recovery was aided by the continuing waves of immigration, which provided both economic demand and the manpower for continued growth. Technology and industrialization were also key factors, especially in communications.

The telegraph, first demonstrated in 1836, now enabled the instantaneous linking of cities. For the newspapers especially, the ability to instantly access stories from far away ensured that not only business and commercial news but also criminal and personal sensationalism did not have to originate locally. The young Frenchman, Alexis deTocqueville, writing his observations from 1835 to 1840, dedicated an entire chapter to the importance of newspapers and noted the "prodigious growth of the press in the United States."

Thanks to its excellent port and connection to the west via the Erie Canal, New York was fast out-distancing other Eastern cities in establishing itself as the nation's commercial capital and population center. Despite the expansion, certain aspects of metropolitan life continued to remain decidedly "small town," as was demonstrated by the sensation attendant on the disappearance and death of a young clerk in a retail cigar store named Mary Cecilia Rogers.

The Mary Cecilia Rogers Case

On Friday, August 6, 1841, Philip Hone, former Mayor of New York City and life-long civic leader, penned the following entry in his diary:

> Friday, Aug. 6 – *Shocking Murder*. The body of a young female named Mary Cecilia Rogers was found on Thursday last in the river near Hoboken, with horrid marks of violation and violence on her person. She was a beautiful girl, an attendant in the cigar shop of John Anderson in Broadway. She left home for a walk on the Sunday previous and was seen near Barclay Street in company with a young man, as if on an excursion to Hoboken; since which no trace of her was found, until the dreadful discovery on Thursday.
>
> She is said to have been a girl of exceeding good character and behavior, engaged to be married, and has no doubt fallen victim to the brutal lust of some of the gang of banditti that walk unscathed and violate the laws with impunity in this moral and religious city. No discoveries have yet been made. Some examinations have taken place, but the parties were proved to have been innocent. Great pains is [sic] taken to find the young man who accompanied the ill-fated girl, but as yet without success.

Although some of Hone's comments probably derived from newspaper accounts, it is evident that he was aware of Ms. Rogers, her place of employment, and the street gangs that preyed on local citizens.

Born in Connecticut in 1820, Mary and her mother, Phoebe, came to New York after her father died in a steamship explosion. Subsequently, they opened a boarding house near lower Broadway at 126 Nassau Street. An extremely pretty girl in the fashion of the times, she came to the attention of John Anderson, a successful and ambitious tobacco merchant who operated a store at 319 Broadway near City Hall.

Anderson's Tobacco Emporium acquired a high degree of notoriety, thanks to the promotional efforts of its proprietor. Located near "newspaper row," City Hall, and the Shakespeare Tavern (a favorite haunt of poets and writers), the back room became an informal meeting place for the powerful and influential. As a result, the Emporium was not infrequently mentioned in newspaper articles.

Hoping to give his male patrons another reason to stop frequently, Anderson hired Mary Rogers as the counter girl after assuring her mother that she would never be left alone in the shop and that she would be escorted home each evening. Before long, her charms were being noted in the newspapers, one of which described her as "a brilliant luminary to catch the butterflies that loved to flutter around so attractive a center." Her popularity was such that when she left home for several hours without telling her mother, the newspapers covered the event as a major disappearance.

Mary's looks and demure manners attracted many men. Among the more serious was Alfred Crommelin who boarded at her mother's house and showed a sincere interest in her. At the time of her disappearance and death, she was thought to be engaged to another young boarder named Daniel Payne who was employed as a cork cutter. Payne's familiarities with Mary so upset Crommelin that he left the boarding house.

Sunday, July 25, 1841, was a hot day in New York with temperatures ascending into the 90s. Rising early, Mary Rogers assisted her mother with breakfast and housekeeping. Shortly before 10:00, she knocked at the door of her fiancé, Daniel Payne, and told him that she planned to visit her aunt. They arranged to meet later in the evening. A late-afternoon thundershower caused Payne and Mrs. Rogers to believe that Mary might have spent the night at her aunt's. When she failed to return the next day, they began a search and, on Monday afternoon, placed a "Missing Persons Notice" in the *New York Sun*.

Across the river from lower New York in Hoboken, New Jersey, was an area then known as the Elysian Fields. Inns and refreshment venues catered to a wide variety of patrons. On the afternoon of Wednesday, July 28th, three young men, wandering near a rock formation known as Sybil's Cave, noticed something floating in the river. Curious, they obtained a scull (a small rowboat) and rode out to investigate. What they discovered was the badly bruised body of a young woman floating on her back, her arms crossed at her chest. Improvising a towline made from a length of rope, they towed the body to shore. A crowd gathered, including, coincidentally, her former admirer, Alfred Crommelin. On seeing the body, he identified it as that of Mary Rogers.

It would be 7:00 p.m. before the authorities could assemble a coroner's inquest and perform an autopsy. The combination of physical injuries and advanced decomposition accelerated by the heat presented serious problems, but the autopsy revealed bruises on the throat consistent with strangulation. On further examination, the coroner, Dr. Richard Cook, discovered that a piece of lace from the women's petticoat had been tightly wound around the neck and knotted. The vaginal area was so bruised that he concluded that Mary Rogers had been "abducted, brutally violated by no fewer than three assailants, and finally murdered." Further evidence showed that her hands had been tied and that, post-mortem, the body had been dragged along the ground. The fact that the bonnet was tied with a slipknot and that the body had been dragged with a hitch seemed to some to indicate that a seaman or sailor might be involved.

The discovery of the body started a media hysteria. Unlike the Jewett case, which immediately pointed to a single suspect, the Rogers murder opened a wide avenue for speculation in every direction. Suspicion initially fell on Daniel Payne, but he provided an airtight alibi, and suspicions fell on others ranging from a young sailor to former patrons of the tobacco shop to local gangs. Not content to stop with the perpetrator of the deed, some of the papers, including James Gordon Bennett's *Herald*, used the crime to strike out at the ineptness of the magistrates and police. As a number of suspects were questioned and released and the authorities drew no closer to resolving the case, speculation and commentary continued at a less accelerated pace.

On August 25th, exactly one month after Mary had embarked on the fatal trip, two boys, looking for sassafras bark in a thicket near Hoboken, discovered various items of women's clothing, including a handkerchief bearing the initials "MR," which they gave to their mother. The boys were the sons of Mrs. Fredericka Loss who ran an inn/tavern called "Nick Moore's House" not far from where Mary's body had been brought ashore. After inexplicably waiting for several days, she turned the items over to the authorities. On questioning, Mrs. Loss recalled serving refreshments to Mary and a "man of dark complexion" at her inn in the late afternoon of Sunday, July 25th, after which they wandered away. She also claimed to have heard a scream later in the evening. Once again, the Rogers case was back in the headlines.

Since the discovery of Mary's body, her presumed fiancé, Daniel Payne, had, according to his brother, spent most of his time in an alcoholic stupor. Having left Mrs. Rogers's boarding house for other quarters, on October 7th, he left his room, stopped at a number of bars, and purchased a vile of laudanum, a powerful opiate. He proceeded to Hoboken and, after drinks at Mrs. Loss's tavern, went to the thicket where the clothing had subsequently been found. He wrote a short note ("To the world, here I am on the very spot. May God forgive me for my misspent life"), placed the note in his pocket, and consumed the drug. While waiting for it to take effect, he stopped at several other taverns and proceeded to the place where Mary's body had been found. There, he laid down and died. The press accounts that followed his suicide depicted the alcoholic cork cutter as a tragic romantic in the high Victorian tradition.

A little more than a year later, another bizarre occurrence revived the case once again. On November 3rd, Mrs. Loss was accidentally shot by one of her sons who was cleaning a shotgun. The wound quickly became septic, and she lay in a delirious state for ten days. In her delirium, she experienced hallucinations, which included the spirit of a young woman standing near the bed. When the physician informed her sons that their mother's case was terminal, they supposedly remarked that "the great secret will come out."

Justice Gilbert Merritt, who had conducted the initial investigation into Mary's death, spent time with the dying Mrs. Loss and also questioned her two sons. Following the inquest, which returned a verdict of accidental death, he summed up his suspicions and, after the death of Mrs. Loss, proceeded to file an affidavit alleging the involvement of her and her sons in the Rogers death. His charges stated, in part, "The said sons and their mother kept one of the most depraved and debauched houses in New Jersey, and that all of them had a knowledge of and were accessory to and became participators in the murder of said Mary C. Rogers and the concealment of her body." Though not specifically stated, Merritt believed that Mary had died while undergoing an abortion at the Nick Moore's House.

At that time, abortion was not uncommon among all social classes. An Englishwoman, Ann Lohman arrived in New York in 1831 and became extremely well known and very wealthy as an abortionist. Styling herself as Madam Restell, she owned a large mansion on Fifth Avenue (referred to as "the mansion built on babies' skulls") where she catered to society women and supposedly maintained branch facilities in various other places for the less well off. Legally considered misdemeanors, abortions were performed by physicians, midwives, and professional practitioners as well.

Shortly after the death of Mrs. Loss, the *Tribune* became the first newspaper to openly surmise that Mary Rogers had died as the result of a "premature delivery." The abortion theory rapidly gained ground as it also would have explained the excessive mutilation in the genital area. In an age when many women died in childbirth—and cleanliness and sterilization were not yet considered essential to surgical procedures—it seemed a reasonable solution. The man seen with Mary was now thought to be her physician/abortionist and, as a result of their involvement, Mrs. Loss's sons were arrested.

These new revelations set off a wave of media madness, as Bennett's *Herald* took issue with the *Tribune* story, and other papers rushed to speculate on whom else might have been involved. Others at first defended Mary's reputation but, ultimately, following an inconclusive hearing for the Loss sons resulting in no criminal charges, most accepted the botched abortion theory. Among others, doubts continued to linger given the obvious evidence of strangulation.

The Mary Rogers case remains unsolved. The disappearance of some key records continues to frustrate modern researchers. Whether they were intentionally removed at the time or lost over the years is unknown, as is the value of any further evidence that might contribute to an ultimate solution. Despite this, the Rogers case, and its media excitement, had far-reaching effects, both locally and in literature.

In the words of one historian, "the drama of Mary Rogers would be one of the earliest and most significant murder cases to play out in the pages of the American press, laying the groundwork for every 'crime of the century' to follow . . . "

In her examination of the case, *The Mysterious Death of Mary Rogers: Sex and Culture in Nineteenth-Century New York*, history professor Amy Gilmar Srebnick comments:

> Through the press, Mary Rogers herself had become a violent and erotic text. Her story pushed at the boundaries of contemporary social discourse while it simultaneously indulged fantasized notions of the erotics of city life and the erotics of death, both significant aspects of antebellum sentimental and popular culture.
>
> Played out first in the penny papers and later in cheap mystery novels, they (the press) expressed beliefs that saw women—or at least those whose sexual or class identity placed them beyond the margins of respectability—as both the source of urban social disorder and sexual danger and at the same time those most endangered.

As a result of the increased public awareness created by the case, New York's abortion law was materially strengthened. The swell of criticism regarding the absence and inefficiency of qualified law enforcement and investigative capability resulted in the demand for an effective and organized police force, which ultimately became law in the 1845 Police Reform Act that created the New York Police Department.

Mary Rogers's legacy was to be further enhanced. As the case unfolded, an impoverished, alcoholic writer/editor who had previously published a successful mystery story, approached his publisher with the idea of presenting a fictionalized account in which his literary detective, C. Auguste Dupin, solved the actual case. In the first draft of the story, the author took the position that Mary (or Marie as she was depicted) was murdered by a gang. Shortly before the concluding installment was to be published, the news broke regarding the probable abortion, and the ending was changed to conform to the more popular solution. The author was Edgar Allan Poe, and his story, *The Mystery of Marie Rogêt*, is thought to be the first example of a fictional mystery based on an actual case. Along with *The Murders in the Rue Morgue* and *The Purloined Letter*, it is considered by critics to be one of the founding works of the detective story. In death, the "beautiful Cigar Girl" not only helped pave the way for municipal reform but achieved literary immortality.

Chapter 3
"Crimes (and Trials) of the Century"

Stanford White—The Time and the Place

The period between the end of the Civil War through the turn of the 20th century has been referred to as the "Gilded Age." The growth that occurred in the United States was responsible for the creation of many new fortunes. In New York City, the older traditional society of "The 400" (so called because social leader Caroline Astor's ballroom had a capacity of 400) was rapidly being invaded or supplanted by the newer fortunes. Devotees of "Conspicuous Consumption," they built increasingly larger and more elaborate mansions along Fifth Avenue and memorialized themselves in public works projects ranging from museums to libraries to fountains and parks. Their comings and goings were avidly watched by a public that regarded them with the degree of interest and awe that later generations would reserve for movie stars. One reason for this had to do with the equation of wealth with virtue.

Public acceptance of the idea that wealth and goodness were intertwined also derived from the fact that, in the days before governmental welfare and entitlement programs, wealthier citizens were often highly visible as community benefactors. Steel magnate Andrew Carnegie, who believed he owed his success to his ability to access books and educate himself, erected libraries—many of which still exist—in communities large and small throughout the United States. Personal collections of artworks, antiques, and historic manuscripts helped to establish world famous museums. Others bequeathed their houses and estates to public usage. Perhaps one of the most important reasons that members of the lower and middle classes viewed the wealthy with approval was that, in the land of opportunity, they aspired to someday join them.

The society that the so-called "Nouveau Riche" built, and in which they moved, was restricted and highly regulated. To be acceptable, one had to live in the right part of the city, spend summer at the right resort, patronize select stores, and consult only approved professionals including doctors, attorneys, and architects. Founded by Charles Follen McKim, William Rutherford Mead and Stanford White, the architectural firm of McKim, Mead & White—high society's first choice in building design—was responsible for many of the era's iconic landmarks, including New York's Manhattan Municipal Building, the Washington Arch, the Pennsylvania (Railroad) Station and, in Washington, D.C., the National Museum of American History and the West and East wings of the White House. Though they worked in many styles, they would become best known for their classical adaptations. (Pennsylvania Station was modeled on the Baths of Caracalla in Rome.)

The firm also designed many elaborate private homes. Stanford White and his friend, sculptor Augustus Saint-Gaudens, not only combined their talents but traveled to Europe, importing whole rooms or important architectural details for installation in their creations. A noted man-about-town and reputed ladies' man, White frequented the haunts of New York's café society. One of the most popular was an entertainment venue on Madison Square in Manhattan that he had designed—the original Madison

Square Garden. No one would have considered it a locale for murder.

The Stanford White Case

The evening of June 26, 1906, saw the opening of a musical review called "Mamzelle Champagne" at the rooftop theatre of Madison Square Garden. Seated alone at a table near the stage was the prominent architect, Stanford White, immediately recognizable by his cropped red hair and ample mustache.

As a singer began a number called "I Could Love a Million Girls," a young man dressed in a long black overcoat approached White's table. Drawing a pistol, he pumped three shots at close range into the architect's face, then turned, removed the bullets from the gun, held the pistol aloft, and walked casually towards the exit.

Near the elevator, one woman recognized the killer as Harry Thaw, son of a prominent Pittsburgh family with multiple business interests and a multi-millionaire. Another woman, stunningly attractive, reacted with shock, "Good God, Harry! What have you done?" asked Evelyn Nesbitt Thaw, the shooter's wife. Thaw replied calmly, "All right, Dearie. I have probably saved your life."

The strange series of events that built to a climax on the roof of Madison Square Garden involved a bizarre love triangle. Evelyn Nesbitt, who became both Stanford White's mistress and Harry Thaw's wife, was born in Pittsburgh in 1884. Her father, an attorney, died when Evelyn was eight and, lacking financial resources, the family lived in hardship. The mother attempted menial work and ran several boarding houses, but with two young children—Evelyn and her younger brother—it was a life of grinding poverty.

As Evelyn approached her teens, her personal beauty became more apparent. In an age that placed a high value on the civilizations of Ancient Greece and Rome and based many of their structures on their architecture, young Evelyn's classic features were perfectly suited to the time. Early into her teens, she embarked on a career as an artist's model and quickly became the major support of her family. When Evelyn was 15, she insisted that the family move to New York so that she could pursue further opportunities. It was a timely move. A major technological advancement that would impact not only her career but also the media coverage that followed White's murder occurred in 1897, when photographic reproduction became available for high-speed presses. Women's fashion magazines seeking the most attractive models paid well, and Evelyn quickly found work. Through the efforts of a theatrical agent, she became a member of the Floradora Sextet—one of the era's most famous and glamorous ensembles. She was quickly noticed by Stanford White who arranged an introduction.

Although he was charming and affable, White's sexual obsession with young, even underage, girls was an unspoken matter of concern to close friends. Introduced to White by another member of the chorus, the three dined at his sumptuous apartment/studio in the tower of Madison Square Garden. On the second floor of the apartment was a large room featuring a red velvet swing that White urged Evelyn to use. Following later lunches and a meeting with her mother, White began to shower the family with attention and gifts. He would ultimately arrange a private dinner with Evelyn in his apartment, after which he plied her with (possibly drugged) champagne and, while she was unconscious, raped her. Though initially upset, Evelyn ultimately became White's willing mistress.

Other men also vied for her attentions, among them the young actor John Barrymore and a mysterious admirer who sent an array of flowers and gifts signed "Mr. Monroe." Eventually, at a party, Mr. Monroe was revealed as Harry K. Thaw. Thaw was the son of a wealthy Pittsburgh family and had a long record of mental instability. He was also possessed of a violent hatred for Stanford White, whom he believed had snubbed him on a social occasion.

Though initially repulsed, Evelyn realized that there was no long-term future with White and, encouraged by her mother, began to accept Thaw's advances. On a trip to Europe with Evelyn and her mother, Thaw continually badgered the girl for details about her relationship with White. When she confessed the truth, he became enraged. Parting from Evelyn's mother, Thaw and the girl proceeded to Germany where he had rented an isolated castle. There, he beat her savagely with a dog whip, and she discovered that he was a heavy drug user.

Once she had returned to New York, Evelyn met again with White who suggested she consult a lawyer to protect her from Thaw. She also discovered that their relationship had cooled and that White was in pursuit of other women. Thaw continually sent gifts and begged her to marry him. Ultimately, he enlisted the aid of his dominating mother who traveled to New York to assure Evelyn that marriage would change her son for the better. They married and moved to Pittsburgh, but given Evelyn's past and Harry's reputation, the couple, despite his wealth, were social outcasts. For Evelyn, familiar with the glamour and notoriety of the stage, it was an especially lonely life.

In March 1906, Harry proposed that he, Evelyn, and his mother make a trip to England. They were set to sail on June 28th. On the evening of June 26th, an exceptionally warm night, they went on to dinner and then to Madison Square Garden for the show, "Mamzelle Champagne." Inexplicably, Harry wore a heavy overcoat, and in his pocket was a gun. Immediately following the shooting, a placid Thaw was taken into custody by police authorities. A reporter for the *New York Evening World* who was present to review the show, ran downstairs and commandeered a telephone. The media circus had begun.

The following day, and for many days thereafter, the city's newspapers headlined the story. It was not long before reporters began unearthing the unsavory details of White's life and sexual tastes. Two days after the murder on June 28th, the *World*, in the multiple headlines typical of the time, revealed the coloration that the coverage would take: "Men in White's set shiver and keep silent," "Not a word in eulogy of dead intimate," and "From millionaire's parties to the morgue." Even the then-new Nickelodeons, precursors of motion pictures, rushed to capitalize on the event, as Edison's studio created a film titled, "Rooftop Murder."

Despite the fact that White was the victim, his status and reputation, coupled with the circumstances of the crime, made him the logical media target, even among journalists who were former friends. James Gordon Bennett cabled his paper, *The New York Herald*, "Give him Hell!" *Vanity Fair* headlined a story, "Stanford White, Voluptuary and Pervert, Dies the Death of a Dog." When a cab man told a *Tribune* reporter, "I knew that fella would be killed sooner or later, but I thought that it would be a father that would do it—not a husband," he correctly anticipated the line that the defense would take—the so-called "unwritten law" defense (a husband is justified in killing his wife's lover). Also involved in the media attention was a group of female reporters, referred to as "the Pity Patrol," assigned to cover the story from the woman's viewpoint. They depicted Evelyn as the young innocent wronged by the evil lecher.

At the trial that would begin the following February, the prosecution team would be headed by District Attorney William Travers Jerome. Although Jerome was, at the time, involved in an illicit relationship with a much younger woman, he announced that he would "tear Evelyn Thaw 'limb from limb' and exhibit the interesting remains triumphantly." Because of the public nature of the crime and the simplicity of the facts of the case, the prosecution called few witnesses. From the beginning, it was obvious that the defense, led by celebrity attorney Delphin Delmas, intended to defame White and implied that Thaw's admittedly irrational behavior resulted from anguish over Evelyn's rape.

The most dramatic moment of the case occurred when Evelyn herself took the stand and, led by Delmas, described her relationship with White up to and including his assault on her. The mysterious apartment, the red velvet swing, and the graphic details of how she was drugged with champagne were all seized on by the media. Jerome's cross-examination was intended to expose Evelyn's past. He brought up her continued associations with White and her involvement with other men. (Though he had subpoenaed John Barrymore, the actor realized that public involvement with the case could cost him his career, and he temporarily disappeared.) Evelyn's confident responses and demure appearance created sympathy, both among the public and among the five members of the jury who found Thaw not guilty by reason of insanity, thus "hanging" the verdict.

A second trial nine months later found Thaw not guilty by reason of insanity and resulted in his commitment to an asylum for the criminally insane in northern New York. It was an optimal solution. The fact that he was acquitted seemed to satisfy many of Evelyn's sympathizers. Those who believed him a deranged murderer were relieved that he would be confined. Thaw would gain release years later. Evelyn embarked on a career in Vaudeville, largely based on her experiences in the case.

Although more than a century has passed since these events transpired, the case has had a lasting effect, both on the public and in the media. Undoubtedly, much of this has to do with the prominence of White's work and the landmark status his buildings have achieved. Multiple books have been written about the case and those involved in it, and a 1955 movie, "The Girl in the Red Velvet Swing," starred Ray Milland as Stanford White and Joan Collins as Evelyn Nesbitt. In 1996, Suzannah Lessard, a great-granddaughter of White, published "The Architect of Desire: Beauty and Danger in the Stanford White Family," in which she describes the disgrace felt by generations of the family over White's actions. Ironically, she would also affirm that his sexual deviations were perpetuated in the behavior of some of his descendants.

The notoriety of the case has attached itself firmly to White's reputation and perhaps even influences, to a degree, the way in which his work is judged. It might be said that just as some of his buildings embody the architectural excesses of the Gilded Age, his life was similarly emblematic of the personal ones.

The Lindbergh Kidnapping—The Time and the Place

When a shocking and horrendous crime is committed against an individual of heroic or celebrity stature in the public mind, an intense amount of pressure builds on both the media and the justice system. As the public demands details of the event, a similar pressure mounts, both on and from the media. Law enforcement authorities are charged with solving the crime in the least amount of time possible. By the time a perpetrator, or perpetrators, has been identified, the media/public mind may well have settled on a verdict, and the nexus of pressure then shifts to the court system.

All of these factors were present in the kidnap-murder of the infant son of Charles and Anne Lindbergh and the subsequent capture, trial and execution of Bruno Richard Hauptmann. In the opinion of Sir Ludovic Kennedy, British journalist, broadcaster and author, and others, all the elements were complicit in facilitating a miscarriage of justice and the death of an innocent man. Other commentators, from those contemporary with the event up to the present, are convinced of Hauptmann's guilt. The truth might lie somewhere in between.

The time between the end of the First World War (November, 1918) and the stock market crash that heralded the Great Depression (October, 1929) was a period of immense technological, economic and social upheaval in the United States. The automobile, thanks to Henry Ford's production methods, became available to millions; the entertainment industry blossomed and the motion picture studio system matured; and commercial radio broadcasting, inaugurated in Pittsburgh in 1921, spread rapidly as nationwide networks came into being.

In its infancy, commercial radio receivers were awkward and expensive, requiring three different types of batteries and costing over $100.00—a large sum in the early to mid-'20s. Programming was scarce, and the receivers required frequent adjustment. Originally, many felt that radio's chief applications would include financial information, cultural events, and educational programs. The advent of more stations, the development of compact inexpensive radios, and the creation of programming formats dedicated to entertainment and news changed that calculus and made it a medium readily accepted by the masses.

Key to radio's ever-growing popularity was its accessibility, immediacy, and low-cost entertainment value. Early programming did not rely on recordings but on live broadcasts of favorite singers, comedians, and dance bands. Hollywood and Broadway stars were often featured in dramatizations of movies and plays in which they were appearing. Major news and sporting events could now be covered live, and newscasters and announcers lent an excitement and immediacy through their unique voices and presentation styles that quickly made themselves celebrities.

In the course of the Great Depression, people who could no longer afford to purchase phonograph records or even newspapers came to rely even more on radio. As prices for radio sets declined to about $5.00, radios' penetration in the American market grew substantially. The power of the relatively new medium was never displayed more vividly than in a tragic crime and trial involving one of the era's greatest heroes and most notable personalities.

The Lindbergh Case

If one year represented the high-water mark of the "Roaring Twenties," it was 1927. Sound came to the movies; the 1927 New York Yankees—considered by many the greatest team ever to play organized baseball— won the World Series; and, in May, a shy, tousled young aviator in a tiny plane became the first to fly non-stop between New York and Paris. His name was Charles Lindbergh.

In the modern world, it is virtually impossible to realize the adulation in which Lindbergh was held following his heroic achievement. On his return, New York held a tickertape parade in his honor. Songs were written about him, and toys and souvenirs bore his likeness. Playing on his boyish appearance, the media idealized Lindbergh as the personification of the young American man, depicting him as friendly and outgoing. The reality was quite different. Extremely reticent and secretive, he came to detest the attention heaped on him. Shortly after his storied flight, he met and married Anne Morrow, daughter of J.P. Morgan partner and American diplomat Dwight Morrow. In 1930, Charles A. Lindbergh, Jr., their first child, was born.

Seeking a home away from the glare of publicity, the couple and their son had just moved into a newly built house in rural Hopewell, New Jersey. There, on March 1st, 1932, the unthinkable happened. Between 8:00 and 10:00 p.m., gaining access to the second-story nursery by means of a ladder, an intruder took the child.

Police were immediately called. On the windowsill in the nursery, Lindbergh spotted an envelope. After it was dusted for fingerprints, it was opened. Inside was a demand for $50,000 in specific denominations. At the bottom was a design consisting of two interlocked circles and three holes. Key misspellings in the note seemed to indicate someone of European—possibly German—origin. Outside the house below the nursery window, police found footprints in the wet ground and indentations made by a ladder. A carpenter's chisel lay near the impressions. A short distance away, the ladder itself was found in three pieces.

Public reaction to the crime was one of shock and anger, and thousands of letters poured in to the makeshift police headquarters in the Lindbergh's garage. Many expressed outrage, some offered prayers and consolation, and others—from cranks—offered theories about the crime or various modes of solving it. All had to be read and sorted.

From early on, the Lindbergh case would be characterized by the many bizarre circumstances, odd characters, publicity seekers, and frauds drawn to it. Offers to solve the case or to assist in recovering the child came from sources as varied as gangster Al Capone, then imprisoned at Atlanta, and Washington socialite and Hope Diamond owner Evelyn Walsh McLean. All were distractions that cruelly raised false hopes in the grieving and anxious parents. The peculiar incident that was to prove true involved an eccentric retired teacher, physical fitness advocate, and self-described patriot named John F. Condon.

Dr. Condon resided in a modest home in the Bronx—the northern-most borough of New York City. Outraged by the crime, he placed an advertisement in a local paper, the *Bronx Home News*, offering to augment the demanded ransom or to act as a go-between. The letter appeared in the March 8th edition of the paper, and on the following day, he received a reply. Written in broken English similar to the ransom note found at the crime scene and containing many misspellings, the letter accepted the offer and included a sealed envelope addressed to Lindbergh. The letter advised that, once the money was obtained, the words "Mony [sic] is redy [sic]," should be placed in the *New York American*.

After discussing the possible next step with a friend, Condon decided to telephone Lindbergh. His call was taken by Robert Thayer, Lindbergh's personal secretary. After presenting his credentials, Condon asked to speak to Lindbergh, who requested that he open and read the letter addressed to him. The second note authorized Condon to act as a go-between and defined the dimensions of the package that should hold the ransom money. It also stated that the child was located 150 miles away.

When Condon described the unique intersecting circles with three dots or holes, Lindbergh knew it was genuine and requested that Condon come to Hopewell. Condon immediately did so, and after discussions, it was decided to place the ad in the newspaper. To disguise Dr. Condon's identity, it would be signed, "Jafsie"—a transliteration of his three initials.

On the day that the "money is ready—Jafsie" ad appeared in the *New York American*, Condon received a telephone call. An accented voice asked if he occasionally wrote for the papers. Condon acknowledged this and was told to stay home evenings between six and midnight, and he would receive another note. In the course of the conversation, the caller spoke to someone else—leading Condon to believe that at least two people were involved.

The following night, a taxi driver delivered a letter setting a time and place for the meeting.

The first meeting arranged between Dr. Condon and the kidnapper(s) was to take place in Woodlawn Cemetery in the Bronx. Condon drove to the site accompanied by his friend, Al Reich, a former prizefighter. As they waited by the cemetery gate, an individual holding a handkerchief to his face walked past the car. Reich believed him to be a lookout. A short time later, a second individual waved a handkerchief from behind the bars of the gate. The man Condon met identified himself only as "John" and assured him that the baby was well. Condon demanded proof, which John agreed to provide. The following day, a package delivered to Condon contained the baby's sleeping suit.

Against the advice of the authorities, Lindbergh agreed to the demands of the kidnapper(s) and, after a subsequent exchange of correspondence, a meeting was arranged. The money selected for the ransom was in two forms: the box defined by the kidnapper(s) would hold $50,000 in Gold Certificates—a printed currency backed by the gold standard. A second package contained $20,000 in silver certificates (conventional currency). The serial numbers of the bills were recorded.

On the night of April 2, 1932, Lindbergh and Condon, following the kidnapper(s)' instructions, arrived at St. Raymond's Cemetery. Seeing no one else, they were about to leave when a voice heard by both called, "Hey, doctor," from inside the cemetery. After preliminary conversation, in which Condon convinced the man to reduce the demand to $50,000, he exchanged the box containing that amount for an envelope. John informed Condon that the baby was being kept on a boat and advised him not to open the envelope for six hours.

On the drive back, Condon opened the note. Written with misspellings similar to the ransom note, it described the child's whereabouts as "on the Boad [sic] Nelly." The location was given as Horseneck Beach and Gayhead near Elizabeth Island. The following day, Lindbergh engaged in a fruitless aerial search for the boat carrying his son.

On May 12th, a truck driver stopping to relieve himself in the woods about a mile from the Lindbergh home discovered the body of a child. Though partially decomposed, certain key identifying features and items of clothing made it possible to confirm the identity as the Lindbergh child. The cause of death was listed as a blow to the head.

Once the baby's body had been found, pressure to find a culprit intensified. Multiple "suspects" were identified and subjected to extremely rigorous questioning. These included servants of the Lindberghs and Morrows (one of whom—a young woman named Violet Sharp—committed suicide in the course of the investigation rather than face further questioning), and even Dr. Condon. Still, no viable suspect emerged.

In the interval following the transfer of the ransom money, bills began to appear irregularly in banks and business establishments, usually in small amounts. The Gold Certificates, which composed the largest part of the ransom, had been recalled by the government in 1933; so, when a gentleman with a German accent presented one at a filling station on September 15, 1934, the clerk recorded the license number and reported it to the police. The number was traced to Bruno Richard Hauptmann, a German-born carpenter residing in the Bronx, and he was subsequently arrested and questioned. The authorities searched his house and, upon dismantling the garage he rented, discovered $14,600 in Lindbergh ransom money. Hauptmann insisted that it had been given to him by a friend who afterward returned to Germany and died there, and that the money he was using was owed him prior to his friend's departure. Throughout an extensive investigation, in the course of which he may have been beaten, Hauptmann provided samples of handwriting and was asked to utter the phrase, "Hey, doctor," in the presence of a disguised Charles Lindbergh. Despite the passage of two years, Lindbergh identified him as the voice of "Cemetery John."

Following an extradition hearing in New York, Hauptmann was returned to Hunterdon County, New Jersey, to face trial in the Flemington Courthouse. The trial was quickly dubbed "The Trial of the Century." From the time of Hauptmann's arrest, the press began a crusade based on the presumption of guilt. Both Hauptmann's nationality and personality put him at a disadvantage. Much of the anti-German prejudice fomented at the time of World War I was still present. Hauptmann's aloof and distant demeanor could easily be construed as arrogance.

Hundreds of reporters from around the country and the world, among them the most notable in their field, descended on the Courthouse. Technicians installed hookups for radio feeds to carry reportage of what journalist and social critic H.L. Mencken called "the greatest story since the Resurrection." In return for his story, the *New York Journal* provided Hauptmann with an attorney, Edward J. Reilly, who spoke in stentorian tones and dressed in full formal attire. He was well past his prime and an alcoholic who frequently drank at lunch. His assistant, C. Lloyd Fisher, was a local attorney with no defense experience. Heading the prosecution was David T. Wilentz, Attorney General of New Jersey. Flamboyant, yet effective, Wilentz clearly saw the trial as a means of furthering his political ambitions.

The trial also attracted thousands of spectators—including souvenir vendors who hawked models of the "kidnap ladder"—and morbid curiosity seekers. Jurors had to run a nightly gauntlet through the crowd as they proceeded to their hotel. It was evident that the mob expected, and demanded, a guilty verdict.

Three primary elements formed the basis for the prosecution's case. The first of these was the $14,600 of Lindbergh ransom money found hidden behind a wall in the rented garage. According to the defense, the money had been left with Hauptmann by a friend and sometime business associate named Isador Fisch who asked him to hold a package until he returned from a trip to Germany. While in Germany, he died of tuberculosis, and Hauptmann later discovered that the package contained cash. He claimed that he had only taken money that he was owed by Fisch.

The prosecution's second most significant evidence, and one that captivated the public imagination, was the kidnap ladder. An expert on wood from the University of Wisconsin named Arthur Kohler testified that wood from the ladder came from Hauptmann's attic. Other portions of the ladder had been traced by police to a lumberyard near Hauptmann's home. Hauptmann, a carpenter by profession, argued that he would never have been associated with the poor workmanship in the ladder.

Following his arrest, Hauptmann had been ordered to transcribe certain words, and at the trial, a team of handwriting experts testified that his handwriting matched that of the ransom notes. Though their credentials and testimony were extremely dubious, the defense failed to aggressively counter those experts and produced only two experts of their own, both unconvincing. The most dramatic moment of the trial occurred when John Condon positively identified Hauptmann as Cemetery John, despite the fact that his earlier descriptions and a police sketch constructed with his input bore no resemblance to the accused.

After 11-1/2 hours of deliberation, the jury unanimously voted Hauptmann guilty, and he was sentenced to death. In the course of the appeals process,

New Jersey Governor Harold Hoffman, who had grave doubts about the case, secretly visited with Hauptmann in an effort to obtain a confession in return for a commutation of the death sentence. His efforts failed, and on April 3, 1936, Hauptmann was executed. In the years following his death, the question of Hauptmann's guilt or innocence has been continuously debated, and multiple theories have been advanced regarding the perpetrators and circumstances of the crime.

Until her death, Hauptmann's widow, Anna, continued to proclaim his innocence and eventually interested Ludovic Kennedy, a British journalist, whose work had resulted in pardons for innocent individuals accused of murder in Britain. In his book about the case, *The Airman and the Carpenter*, he cited multiple inconsistencies, including the dubious qualifications of the State's "expert" witnesses, the pressure on Condon to positively identify Hauptmann, and the creation and planting of evidence by the police, the prosecution and the press. Many of his conclusions were built on an earlier work by Anthony Scaduto, *Scapegoat: The Lonesome Death of Bruno Richard Hauptmann*.

In 2012, Robert Zorn published a book (*Cemetery John: the Undiscovered Mastermind of the Lindbergh Kidnapping*) based on the reminiscences of his father, Eugene C. Zorn, who as a young man was a resident of the Bronx at the time of the kidnapping. On one occasion, the senior Mr. Zorn accompanied a neighborhood resident and acquaintance of German extraction on an excursion to New Jersey, in the course of which he met with two other men, one of whom he later identified as Bruno Richard Hauptmann. The trio engaged in a conversation in German in which the young man heard reference to "Englewood"— the Morrow home where the Lindberghs and their baby were living at the time. Following the kidnapping, the acquaintance, a man named John Knowle, a delicatessen clerk, suddenly had enough money to take a luxurious vacation in Germany.

Working to substantiate his father's belief that John Knowle and his brother, Walter, were involved with Hauptmann in the kidnapping, Mr. Zorn submitted samples of Knowle's handwriting (on envelopes that had been given to Zorn Sr. for his stamp collection) to qualified handwriting experts. Upon comparing them with the original ransom notes, the experts declared them to be of the same hand. Other experts in forensic pathology and criminal profiling likewise expressed support for the involvement of John Knowle in the case. Significantly, a photograph of Knowle bears a striking resemblance to the police artist's sketch of Cemetery John based on Condon's description.

In defining the crime as a conspiracy rather than the work of a single individual, it is possible to resolve many of the discrepancies that caused investigators and writers to seek to exonerate Hauptmann. Perhaps most important, it serves as an exceptionally vivid example of the way in which the mechanisms of justice under pressure from the media and the public can be subverted into providing a convenient narrative rather than pursuing an extensive, if difficult, investigation. The number of books, articles, radio and TV programs, and movies that have appeared in the years following the case reflect an ongoing belief among many that the Lindbergh kidnapping has never been completely solved. Like other celebrated cases such as Jack the Ripper and the Kennedy Assassination, the media, and the public, will continue the quest to resolve what may well be unsolvable.

Part II
A (Public) Taste for Violence

Introduction

The news and entertainment media are dependent for their financial survival on attracting and retaining the interest of the public, so both maintain a high degree of sensitivity to features or cases that attract the most interest. Because of its horrific nature, violent crime and those who perpetrate it have the greatest potential for attracting an audience. Within that category, certain specific types of crime and criminals stand out.

Serial murders—especially those with a bizarre sexual component—hold an especial public fascination. There is nothing particularly new about serial murder. From Gilles de Rais (known as "Bluebeard"), who slaughtered children in 15th century France, to the Harpe brothers, who robbed and killed on the American frontier in the late 18th century, there have always been individuals who for different reasons engaged in multiple murder. Thankfully, the incidence of serial murders and murderers is not large, despite their exaggerated number in books, movies, and on television.

Part of the fascination is due to the fact that serial murderers lend themselves well to dramatic plotting. In addition to the usual police vs. the killer element, there is the added suspense of when, whom and for what reason he will strike again, and how many more victims will be discovered before he is finally caught. This preoccupation with the perpetrator may also be due to the fact that his or her victims tend to be vulnerable, approachable, and less pitied or grieved for by society because of their social status, race or ethnicity, or behavior. A switch in focus on the victims, their typology, their habits and activities may reveal much about the killer.

In actual cases, many serial murderers are detected only after their arrest for a single crime, following which their careers emerge in retrospect. This is true of both John Wayne Gacy and Jeffrey Dahmer. In other situations, the discovery of a number of bodies seeming to fit a similar profile, or contact by witnesses or by the killers themselves, can engage the authorities in a real-time race against the clock. The horror of the crimes and the suspense involved in the pursuit and capture of the perpetrator ensures that serial killers will remain a far larger population in the entertainment world than their actual numbers in reality.

Another aspect of crime favored by the media and the public is the "celebrity case." A murder, an assault, or even a drunk-driving incident that would be relegated to a minor mention in the news—if at all—will receive international coverage if a celebrity is involved, either as a perpetrator or a victim. To an extent, the public attraction to celebrity and celebrities has to do with psychology. Society looks upon celebrities as superior individuals. The gifted athlete, the beautiful actress, and the billionaire businessperson are all viewed as individuals whose extraordinary endowments set them apart from the general population. Because they are followed by the media or, in the case of athletes and entertainers, are professionally a part of it, we can begin to feel that we know them as individuals. We "spend time" with them. We know their faces, voices, and more details about their personal lives than we know about our close neighbors. In an age of information overload, they have become pseudo acquaintances—even if their public face is largely the result of a press agent's efforts.

An unfortunate byproduct of this coverage is the "stalker" effect, whereby an unbalanced individual comes to believe that he or she shares a special relationship with a public figure who is acknowledging them through secret signs or messages. This "star stalking" may be extremely annoying and intrusive, as with Margaret Mary Ray who identified herself as David Letterman's wife and her son as David Letterman, Jr. She broke into Letterman's house in New Canaan, Connecticut, on multiple occasions and also drove his Porsche about town. She eventually committed suicide in 1988 after nearly a decade of pursuing the talk show host.

Celebrity stalking taken to the extreme by delusional, obsessive fans can also result in the death of the object of adoration, as was the case for actress Rebecca Schaeffer who was shot point blank in the chest on her doorstep by a frustrated stalker named Robert John Bando. She had just received her first big break in the sitcom "My Sister Sam." Once any individual attains "superstar" status, the incidence of stalkers, death threats, and other forms of undesired attention, is inevitable. This effect is magnified when the individual intentionally courts publicity.

O.J. Simpson was a superb athlete. Following his extraordinary football career, he remained in the public eye through movie appearances and in television commercials. To the public, he appeared to be an affable, approachable individual with an engaging smile and a ready sense of humor. The circumstances surrounding the murder of his wife, Nicole, and her friend, Ronald Goodman, including a car chase televised as it occurred and a trial that became a major television event, was to epitomize the downside of superstardom.

Although much about John Gotti's day-to-day life was intensely private, the public could believe that they knew him—or at least the type of person he was—through the multiple movies and television portrayals of gangsters and Mafia dons extending back to the 1930s. His own thirst for publicity may well have caused Gotti to attempt to live up to what he believed was expected of him, a fantasy that the media helped create. What he might not have realized is that, at the end of the movie or the program, the gangster never wins.

Violence visited on children has always been especially abhorrent in the civilized world. When that violence is committed by a child or young person within the precinct of a school or learning institution, it is seen as doubly barbaric, in that the deed was perpetrated on the young people not by an outsider but by one of their own and in a locale regarded as safe and secure. Such an act violates so many social tenets that both the media and the public are compelled to question multiple aspects of society, culture, family, and the immediate surroundings in a search to answer, "Why did this happen?" For some questions, regrettably, there are no answers.

Chapter 4
Serial Killers—A Fatal Fascination

In the popular culture, serial killers are *objets de fascination*—objects of fascination—because of their characteristic violent and predatory behavior. Some have even acquired folk hero status. Indeed, for most people, the term "serial killer" conjures up an evil monster with an insatiable lust for sex, torture, and murder.

The reality is more complex. While many, if not most, serial killers are murderers who delight in the act of killing and derive sexual gratification from torturing their victims, in some cases the deaths are incidental to other crimes. For some, robbery and financial gain are the primary motives. Others kill to avoid recognition or subsequent identification—especially following sex crimes. So-called "angels of death" kill for reasons including the altruistic objective of relieving suffering, for the illusion of power, or because of mental delusions.

The serial killer is not a new phenomenon. Gilles de Rais, a fifteenth century knight and companion-in-arms of Joan of Arc, was an insatiable pedophile who may have been responsible for the deaths of hundreds of children. Gilles developed a ritual torture in which he would dress his little victims in fine clothes, get them drunk, sexually victimize them and then hang or stab them. After they were dead, he would dismember or decapitate them. His life inspired Charles Perrault's story of Bluebeard (1697).

America's first-known serial killers were the Harpe brothers. Known as "Big Harpe" and "Little Harpe," in the 1790s they roamed the Tennessee/Kentucky area as far west as southern Illinois, robbing and killing travelers. From time to time, they associated with the river pirates who robbed early settlers traveling the Ohio River. They may have killed as many as 300 people before they were eventually caught and executed by local citizens.

Perhaps the most notorious, and prolific, serial killer of the 19th century was a confidence man named Herman Mudgett, who later styled himself as Dr. Henry Howard Holmes (H.H. Holmes). Though trained as a physician, his proclivities led him into various rackets involving everything from real estate to patent medicine. In 1886, in Chicago, he was employed at the drugstore of Dr. E.S. Holton. Ultimately, he bought the business and subsequently killed Holton's widow.

The drugstore was commercially successful, and Holmes purchased the lot across the street on which he erected a business block known locally as the "Castle." The Castle combined retail space on the first floor with hotel rooms and a variety of windowless chambers and wandering halls above. On the second floor, near his personal office, Holmes had a large bank vault installed. Inside the vault, a chute led to the basement where a glass-bending furnace was installed. After killing his victims, Holmes cremated them in the furnace. As a result, it became impossible to calculate an accurate tally of his victims, which included employees (whom he had previously insured), hotel guests, romantic interests, and customers.

Following the 1893 World's Fair, Holmes left Chicago and returned to the confidence game. When an insurance fraud involving murder went bad, he was arrested. Police investigations led to revelations about his background, and he was subsequently convicted and hanged.

These early crimes remind us that serial murder is not a 20th or 21st century phenomenon, even though the modern media has made it appear so. Likewise, serial murder is not a frequent occurrence but rather a rarity among all homicides, and indeed all crimes. The public obsession may have to do with the later, more sensational "real life" cases that established serial murder in the general consciousness. The cases of Ted Bundy, Jeffrey Dahmer, and John Wayne Gacy will live in memory because of the intimate details with which the public became acquainted.

Thanks to the immediacy of television, we were able to follow the Bundy trial in real time. Even after his conviction and sentencing, interviews that he granted to clergymen seeking to dissuade others from his path were televised. At his execution, cameras placed us among the crowds outside the prison.

The same was true with the Dahmer case: We were able to stand with the curious outside his apartment as the gruesome details became known; we saw the plastic barrel of acid in which he dissolved parts of his victims wheeled out on a dolly. Local residents, aware of the media presence, played to it. One man was found scattering bones from pork ribs on the lawn in an effort to heighten the macabre scene.

Similarly, as police carefully and completely demolished the home of John Wayne Gacy, we were able to watch from street level and occasionally through helicopter shots—an unprecedented view for witnesses.

Overall, just as certain individuals find themselves identifying with characters in a television series to the extent that they believe they know them as people, the extensive immediate and ongoing coverage of a serial killer, his victims and his world can produce a similar effect. Willingly or not, it becomes a real-life drama from which we cannot turn away.

For today's news media, serial murder satisfies the newsworthiness criteria because of its aspects of unusualness, inconceivability, and horror. The media is well aware that serial murders attract readership and viewership, especially in cases involving the serial lust killer. For instance, the case of Jeffrey Dahmer created a financial windfall for the *Milwaukee Journal/Sentinel* with record circulation and sales figures. The increased demand derives from the public's morbid curiosity as to how someone could cold-bloodedly murder over and over again with no remorse. They likewise thrill to the vicarious experience of learning all the horrifying details in the safe confines of their own homes.

To an extent, serial killers tend to be glorified in the media. They have been described as clever, sly, resourceful and even charming—able to elude capture for an inordinately lengthy period of time. In Great Britain, for example, the centennial of the Jack the Ripper murders was celebrated with tee shirts, mugs, and buttons.

Unlike other homicide victims, the victims of serial killers may be chosen by reason of their mere presence and availability or by some characteristic that caused them to be noticed. To this end, the physical appearance, lifestyle, or personal choices of the victim can put them at risk for violent victimization. Prostitutes, for instance, frequently accompany strangers to hidden locations. This makes them relatively easy to access and be preyed upon. In the United States, as many as three-quarters (78.7%) of female victims of serial killers have been prostitutes.

Other common targets include vagrants, the homeless, migrant workers, homosexuals, missing children, single women, college students, elderly women, and hospital patients. The primary characteristics that many victims share are vulnerability, accessibility and, often, anonymity. The serial murderer must gain control over his victim as quickly as possible, drawing the least amount of attention to himself. For example, Jeffrey Dahmer would offer money in exchange for sexually explicit photos of his intended victims taken in his apartment. Coercion could have been used, but it made a lot more sense to gain the victim's trust or to persuade him to come along willingly.

Ted Bundy—The Time and the Place

The America of the 1970s was a divided nation. The Generation Gap and the Vietnam War paved the way for youthful rebellion. A college education, once reserved for the privileged, was now seen as a necessity, and campuses were flooded with students.

Extensive changes were taking place in the popular culture. Starting in the mid-'60s, the Beatles launched a sound that would revolutionize popular music. The drug culture with its psychedelic ramifications became a fixture, first throughout the counter-culture community, then among the young, as media figures such as Harvard professor Timothy Leary encouraged experimentation. The advent of birth control and the Women's Liberation Movement set the stage for what would be called the Sexual Revolution.

For many young women, especially those who had been raised in a sheltered environment, the college experience was both exciting and confusing. In the collegial campus atmosphere, it was easy to miss the fact that among fellow students, friends and teachers, there were predators. One of the worst was a clean-cut, handsome and intelligent young man named Ted Bundy.

The Ted Bundy Case

Bundy, one of the best known serial killers, killed at least 20 young women and possibly as many as 30 between 1973 and 1978 in Washington, Oregon, Utah, Colorado, and Florida. The newsworthiness of the Bundy case derived from his brutal physical and sexual assault of his victims, and the added element of necrophilia. White, female college students with long hair parted in the middle were his preferred victim type, and some reports alleged that Bundy's victims resembled a former girlfriend who callously broke his heart. Bundy vehemently denied that he chose them because of their similarity in appearance.

According to most accounts, Bundy was a manipulative individual. However, as former coworker Ann Rule related in her book, *The Stranger Beside Me*:

Ted was never as handsome, brilliant or charismatic as crime folklore has deemed him. . . . A virtual nonentity before he was suspected of a series of horrific crimes, he somehow became all of those things as the media embraced him. (Rule, 2009, xii)

Rule and Bundy worked as crisis counselors in 1971 answering hotlines at the Seattle Crisis Clinic while Bundy was a psychology student at the University of Washington. They became close friends and shared confidences. Rule described Bundy as "evincing a genuine caring for others" and as one who would listen with full attention to the callers.

Bundy graduated with a degree in Psychology in 1972 and then began law school at the University of Washington. He eventually transferred to the University of Utah Law School in 1973. Using his knowledge of psychology, Bundy was able to disarm many of his victims. For example, he would use a sling or crutches, feign helplessness and request assistance from his intended victim. Another ploy involved the use of a fake police badge to trick his victim into getting into his car. He undoubtedly knew that jurisdictional boundaries would hamper police investigation of his crimes, so he killed women in multiple states.

In August of 1974 in Washington's Sammamish State Park, the remains of several missing girls were found and two were later identified. Police questioned visitors to the park, some of whom described an individual named "Ted" who wore his arm in a sling and who had approached them for help. The odd fact that Bundy always gave his real first name to his potential victims helped police to zero in on him. The "Ted story" became big news across the Pacific Northwest and eventually on a national level.

On November 8, 1974, Bundy tried to kidnap a young woman from a shopping mall in Utah. She escaped and was able to provide police with a description of her attacker and his tan Volkswagen. After first being arrested and convicted of attempted kidnapping in Utah, and then being charged with murder in Colorado, Bundy managed to escape twice. Unfortunately, his second escape resulted in the deaths of several more victims when he bludgeoned and strangled to death three college students at the University of Florida—Tallahassee. Less than one month later, Bundy killed his last victim, a twelve-year-old girl from Lake City, Florida. The four-year killing spree that originated in Washington, and continued in Utah and Colorado, finally ended in Florida when he was caught in a stolen Volkswagen bug.

The Bundy murder trials were among the most publicized trials of the decade. They were televised with Bundy acting as his own attorney, cross-examining many of the state's witnesses, including victims of his attempted abductions. Reporters referred to them as "full-fledged circuses." Ann Rule, who attended the trials, described the "frantic activity [of the press] with three dozen closed circuit television sets blaring out every word of the trial and stations from Colorado, Utah, Washington, and Florida establishing their territory."

In the center of it all was the ring master or the "golden boy" (his self-designation) playing out his command performance to the media, the courtroom, and the bevy of young, female fans ("Ted's groupies") seated directly behind the defense table. According to one reporter:

> Very much aware of the television cameras and other media, he displayed the full range of his complex personality from his charm, intelligence and wit to his ego, temper and contempt for authority. (Boynton, 2004, 267)

In the end, it was all to no avail. Bundy was found guilty and convicted in both of his trials and sentenced to death. He would spend his years on death row still granting interviews with the press, spending hours giving his opinions, theories, and feelings. As the day of his execution approached, the media interest ignited once more. The media circus continued even on the day of his death. He was electrocuted on January 24, 1989, amid a carnival-like atmosphere outside the prison.

Jeffrey Dahmer—The Time and the Place

The collegiate world in which Ted Bundy and his victims lived was largely familiar to the public. The dark netherworld of Jeffrey Dahmer encompassed another social segment altogether. By the 1980s and '90s, Milwaukee, Wisconsin, like many industrial cities of the Middle West, had fallen on hard times. Long known for its output of beer and machinery, the city had seen most of the breweries and industrial plants move out or close.

Immediately west of the heart of downtown is the home of Marquette University, one of the Midwest's notable centers of learning. Outside the urban campus, however, the area includes a diverse mix of the less-than-affluent. Ethnically integrated, the neighborhood—once home to beer barons and industrial magnates—includes fixed-income seniors, the marginally employed, and the poor. It is also the site of the lower end of the city's sex trade. Prostitutes, both male and female, can be found on street corners and in the bars and after-hours clubs.

Populated by such a diverse mix, the locale has long presented a problem to police. Aware that careers can be destroyed by accusations of racial or sexual prejudice, officers on patrol tended to adopt a "live and let live" attitude toward all but overt or violent criminal activity. An after-dark world of transient residents and visitors and anonymous paid sex, it became the ideal hunting ground for Jeffrey Dahmer.

The Jeffrey Dahmer Case

Jeffrey Dahmer's murders spanned three decades—the 1970s, 1980s, and the 1990s—in Milwaukee. The newsworthiness of the Dahmer case centered on serial murder with the added macabre elements of lobotomies, zombeism, cannibalism, and necrophilia. In fact, Dahmer's crimes were eerily similar to those of another Wisconsin case—that of Ed Gein in the 1950s. Author Robert Bloch's story about Norman Bates (*Psycho*, 1959), a character based on Gein, inspired Hitchcock's thriller of the same name. Gein dismembered the bodies of his victims and collected their body parts for a variety of uses, e.g. their skin was stretched into lampshades and "drums." In a similar fashion, Dahmer also violated the corpses of his victims and collected their body parts, mainly their skulls and penises.

Seventeen murders were officially attributed to Dahmer, although the actual number may be higher. His victims consisted largely of Black male homosexuals (a number of whom were prostitutes) who frequented the bars that Dahmer cruised looking for victims. For the most part, they went willingly to his apartment where Dahmer gave them a drink laced with the sedative Halcyon and then strangled them while they were unconscious. A necrophiliac who had sex with and photographed the corpses, he also dismembered his victims and saved some of their body parts as remembrances.

Dahmer operated relatively undetected for over three decades despite contact with police. In the most notorious incident, a 14-year-old victim named Konerak Sinthasomphone escaped from Dahmer. Responding to a concerned resident, police found the drugged and incoherent Sinthasomphone staggering in the street by Dahmer's apartment. Dahmer arrived at the scene and convinced the police that the two were lovers and that Sinthasomphone was drunk. The officers escorted both parties back to Dahmer's apartment where they saw Sinthasomphone's clothes and photographs of him in black bikini briefs. Once the officers left, Dahmer strangled and dismembered the boy. The police officers in the case subsequently were widely criticized for not asking for identification from the boy or Dahmer, who was on probation for sexual assault of a child at the time.

The next contact with police occurred when police officers on patrol encountered an African American male (Tracy Edwards) with handcuffs dangling from his wrist. He told them about a "weird dude" who had handcuffed him. The officers accompanied Edwards to Dahmer's apartment. An officer went to retrieve the key for the handcuffs which Dahmer indicated was in the bedroom and was horrified to find pictures of dismembered bodies, skulls, and a skeleton hanging from a showerhead. Dahmer was immediately arrested and the bizarre tale unraveled.

The Dahmer case became the subject of intense local and national media coverage and achieved mass media and tabloid celebrity. Dahmer and those most visibly involved in his trial, including news reporter Anne Schwartz, defense attorney Jerry Boyle, and District Attorney E. Michael McCann, became local and national celebrities.

One negative effect of the excessive coverage was media interference in the investigation of the case. The media camped outside Dahmer's apartment, reported every movement of the police, and badgered police officials for information. Interviews with locals and neighbors created other problems.

Dahmer's trial began on January 22, 1992. Dahmer chose to plead guilty but insane. The jury declared him fit to stand trial. As compared to the extensive coverage during the investigation, the televised trial of Jeffrey Dahmer was almost anticlimactic. At his trial, Dahmer's defense attorney Jerry Boyle addressed the jury with these remarks:

> You're going to hear about things you probably didn't know existed in the real world. You're going to hear about sexual conduct before death, during death, and after death.

However, any titillating aspects of the case were lost in the hours of expert testimony. The sheer number of crimes and victims' names made the judicial ritual numbing and confusing to watch. In the words of writer Mark Pizzato:

> The courtroom show itself was not very dramatic. The tragic terror of the victims never appeared on screen, only an enigmatic photograph of each one smiling for the camera. None of the photos taken by Dahmer of his victims was shown on TV nor was the other evidence he left. Dahmer himself appeared in the courtroom in a mild-mannered mask, despite his claim of insanity, while witnesses read confession statements and used esoteric psychiatric terms. (Pizzato, 1999, 105)

The trial was basically a battle of "psychiatrists; with those for the defense testifying about Dahmer's mental illness; and those hired by the prosecution testifying about his insanity." After jurors deliberated for a little more than five hours, Dahmer was found legally sane and guilty on all fifteen murder counts. On February 14, 1992, he was sentenced to fifteen consecutive life sentences, requiring him to serve 936 years before being eligible for parole (Wisconsin does not have a death penalty).

His preference for black victims was avenged when he was murdered in prison by an African American inmate named Christopher Scarver on November 28, 1994.

John Wayne Gacy—The Time and the Place

Beginning in the 1970s, a number of talented authors including Stephen King and Peter Straub revived public interest in the horror genre. Though horror stories, movies, and comics have long been available, they were typically heavily stylized. The stories frequently took place in remote locales and in the distant past. By setting their novels and movies in the immediate present, the new generation of writers and directors opened the possibility that blood-curdling experiences didn't require a castle in faraway Transylvania or a tomb in Egypt. They could occur in broad daylight in a suburban neighborhood.

To the residents of Norwood Park, Illinois, the horror was to become reality. The home of John Wayne Gacy was not unlike others in the neighborhood. A single-story brick-faced ranch, it was home to an affable, heavyset man who ran a small construction and remodeling business. Active in civic affairs, he liked to entertain children in costume and makeup as Pogo the Clown. What his neighbors wouldn't know until much later was that beneath the house and on the property were the graves of 28 murder victims; and beneath the clown's makeup was a monster more terrible than any fictional creation.

As the children of the post-war baby boom grew into adolescence, a distressing social trend emerged in the vastly increased number of runaway children. "Running away from home," or seriously considering it, has long been recognized as a facet of adolescence. The sudden wave of teenage runaways that occurred in the 1970s, however, is attributable to a number of causes, including the so-called Generation Gap (the gap in age between much older parents and their children), the emergent youth culture, higher rates of divorce and attendant dysfunctional families, increased mobility, and extensive coverage in the media.

News broadcasts, programs, and magazine and newspaper articles highlighting areas such as New York's East Village and San Francisco's Haight-Ashbury District may have convinced many young people that there was a ready-made support structure to which they could attach themselves. Popular music and the youth-oriented media frequently depicted life within those areas as offering freedom, emancipation, and happiness through the combination of "sex, drugs, and rock 'n' roll."

As the number of teenage runaways increased, concerned parents and relatives were frequently met with skepticism bordering on hostility when they attempted to file Missing Persons Reports at local police departments. Deluged with requests and strapped for resources, many police authorities affected a casual attitude or instituted policies requiring a more extensive amount of time missing before officially filing a report. This would prove to be extremely unfortunate as, in kidnapping and abduction cases, the danger increases exponentially with the passage of hours. It was only through the emergence of a number of high-profile cases such as the 1981 abduction and murder of Adam Walsh, and his father's persistence in solving the case (he was later to become host of the TV program, "America's Most Wanted"), that the media, and consequently public attention, became focused on the problem.

Long before that, the pimps, molesters, and other predators who sought to exploit young runaways had established themselves as regular fixtures around urban bus stations and train depots. Many young people, far from home and confused, were met by ostensibly kind strangers who would ultimately lure them into prostitution or other forms of victimization.

A number of young men getting off the bus at the Chicago terminal would meet a heavyset non-descript looking man who would strike up a conversation and, perhaps, offer them a job in his construction business. Unlike many of the pimps, obvious by their flashy dress and gold chains, John Wayne Gacy's ordinariness was an ideal cover for his sinister motives.

The John Wayne Gacy Case

Serial killer John Wayne Gacy, called the "killer clown," was a performing clown at neighborhood children's parties and other community events. Beneath this public image was a serial murderer who delighted in the torturous acts committed on his victims and the bizarre burial of their corpses in a crawl space under his house. Gacy murdered at least 33 young White boys between 1972 and 1978, preying on homosexuals, male prostitutes, and his own employees in the Chicago area. Gacy would entice the boys with promises of jobs, alcohol, or drugs, then gain control by covering their mouths with a chloroform-soaked rag and assaulting them.

Gacy was married to his first wife and the father of two children when he was convicted of sodomizing a child, at which time he was ordered to undergo a psychiatric evaluation. Two doctors concluded that he had an antisocial personality disorder and was unlikely to benefit from treatment and that he was competent to stand trial. He was sentenced to ten years at the Iowa State Men's Reformatory but served only 18 months before he was paroled. His wife divorced him while he was imprisoned.

Upon release from prison in 1970, Gacy moved to Chicago to stay with his mother and worked as a short order cook. He was again charged with the sexual assault of a teenage boy. The complaint was dismissed when the youth failed to show up at the proceeding. With financial help from his mother, Gacy bought a house in Norwood Park, Chicago. He also married his second wife, Carole, a divorcee with two daughters, a short time later. They would divorce within a few years supposedly due to Gacy's late night carousing with young boys and her discovery of his homosexual magazines.

In 1972, Gacy started his own construction company, PDM (Painting, Decorating and Maintenance) Construction, out of his home. The company was successful and Gacy expanded to remodeling and landscaping. He projected the image of a hardworking businessman and good citizen through his involvement in the Junior Chamber of Commerce and as precinct captain of the Democratic Party. He met and was photographed with First Lady Rosalind Carter in 1978 when he was an organizer of Chicago's annual Polish Constitution Day Parade.

Gacy used his construction business to attract young men looking for jobs, many of whom would later become his victims. He also cruised the bars, the bus terminal, and a park in North Chicago known as a hangout for homosexuals and male prostitutes, often using a fake police badge to lure his victims to his car. At his residence, the victims were persuaded to put on handcuffs and were exposed to a "rope trick," whereby a rope was looped around the victim's neck, knotted twice and then tightened like a tourniquet with a stick. Gacy liked to be in complete control over his powerless, helpless victims.

The police were again alerted to Gacy when two young men who had worked for him were reported missing. Gacy was questioned and his house was searched. The officers located a crawl space beneath his home and noticed an offensive order but could not immediately determine its origin. Based on evidence obtained from the search, including two driver's licenses and several rings (one a high school ring with engraved initials), the police obtained a second search warrant, entered the crawl space, and conducted soil tests. Starting with the point of entry and proceeding through the property, they uncovered 27 bodies. According to Gacy, other victims had been thrown into the nearby Des Plaines River. As the body count began to rise, the Gacy home became a familiar image on national news.

Gacy's defense at trial was that he was insane when he committed the crimes and unable to control his conduct and sought to bolster his insanity plea by explaining that there were actually four johns: John the Contractor, John the Clown, John the Policeman, and 'Jack' the Evil Killer. He was diagnosed by one of the defense psychiatrists, Dr. R.G. Rappaport, as having "a borderline personality organization with the subtype of psychopathic personality and with episodes of an underlying paranoid schizophrenia." Nonetheless, after a six-week criminal trial, Gacy was found guilty on all charges and two days later was sentenced to death.

Gacy would spend fifteen years on death row, filing numerous appeals. While there, he painted canvases of clowns and sold them to help fund his letter writing campaign to over 23,000 people. Toward the end, Gacy denied everything and claimed innocence. On May 10, 1994, he was executed by the State of Illinois.

Serial murderers continue to obsess the press and the general public. Their heinous acts and evil personas captivate and enthrall us all. There may be some truth in the following statement by John Wayne Gacy in a personal communiqué to Dr. Steven Eger in 2003:

> Nearly 80% of what is known about me is from the media, it is they who made this infamous celebrity fantasy monster, and now they have to live with that as I have not granted any interviews in over ten years to media people, . . . (John Wayne Gacy in a personal communiqué to Dr. Steven Eger, 2003, 86).

The media has contributed to the mythology surrounding serial murder by sensationalizing and intensely focusing on every lurid detail. The public also shares responsibility for mythologizing such murderers in its eagerness to absorb any tidbit of information about them.

Ted Bundy became something of a folk hero. In 1977, after Bundy escaped from a Colorado prison, a folk singer in Aspen wrote and sang a salute to "the mighty Bundy." His story was made into two television movies, "The Deliberate Stranger" with actor Mark Harmon (1986), and "Ted Bundy" with actor Michael Reilly Burke (2002). Countless books have also been written about him, including *The Stranger Beside Me, Bundy: The Deliberate Stranger,* and *The Only Living Witness.* He attracted legions of female fans, many of whom corresponded with him in prison.

Several books were also written about Jeffrey Dahmer, including *Milwaukee Massacre, Jeffrey Dahmer: An Unauthorized Biography of a Serial Killer, The Man Who Could Not Kill Enough: The Secret Murders of Milwaukee's Jeffrey Dahmer,* and *Milwaukee Murders:*

Nightmares in Apt. 213. Movies were also made about the story of his life, including "The Secret Life: Jeffrey Dahmer" (1993) and "Dahmer" (2002) with Jeremy Renner in the leading role as Dahmer.

John Wayne Gacy is also the subject of many books, including *The Man Who Killed Boys, The John Wayne Gacy Story,* and *A Passing Acquaintance.* He once bragged to a reporter about the number of books and news articles written about him. Two television movies were also produced about this serial killer, "Gacy" and "To Catch A Killer" with Brian Dennehy as Gacy.

News articles and books will continue to be written, and movies will continue to be made to sell information and to make money. And, we will continue to consume this information in our quest to better understand the rationales underlying this inexplicable behavior. Television and films will perpetuate the fatal fascination with shows and movies based on both actual and fictional cases.

Of course, the reality might well be that serial killers can never be truly understood. The variety of reasons driving them, combined with the complexity of the multiple pathologies they exhibit, probably puts them, as a group, beyond the reach of reasonable cognition. What is fortunate for us is that, thanks to the electronic linkage now available to law enforcement authorities throughout the country and around the world, profiles in victimology, methodology, behavior, and criminal history can assist in identifying these individuals and removing them from society earlier than was previously possible. Likewise, the public's morbid fixation might have a positive side in increasing awareness of the fact that such obsessed killers do not just dwell in the shadows, but walk freely among us.

Chapter 5
School Mass Murders as Major Media Events

What some authorities define as the pressure of an increasingly complex society may well be a contributing factor to the mass murders perpetrated by unbalanced individuals in a variety of venues, including post offices, office buildings, work places, and fast-food restaurants. Nonetheless, mass murder incidents in schools seem more shocking and unsettling. It may be the realization that our educational institutions are no longer sacrosanct and/or that elementary school, high school, and college students may be capable of cold-blooded murder. The killings contradict our assumptions about young adulthood, childhood, innocence, and good and evil.

The various media have been focused on several incidents of school mass murder in the last few decades as particularly newsworthy and as evidence of a violent trend in school crime in modern society. The school shootings by Kip Kinkel at Thurston High School and Mitchell Johnson and Andrew Golden at Westdale Middle School in 1998, the Columbine High School shootings in 1999, and the shootings at Virginia Tech in 2007 are examples.

However, mass killings in schools and on college campuses are not a recent phenomenon. In 1966, Charles Whitman, a 25-year-old student, set up a sniper position in a tower on a University of Texas campus and gunned down 45 people, killing 14. The 1970s and 1980s likewise were not devoid of school shootings. In 1979, a teenage girl named Brenda Spencer killed two adults and wounded eight children and a police officer at an elementary school in San Diego, California. In 1989, a 26-year-old named Patrick Purdy opened fire upon an elementary school playground in Stockton, California. He killed five children and wounded 29 others, as well as a teacher.

Several researchers have described the more recent "spate" of school shootings as a "moral panic," growing out of the horrific actions of deviant individuals (in this case juvenile perpetrators) that cause harm to society overall. For many, if not most, in the media and the political arena, the primary implication of school shootings is that the social order is breaking down and something needs to be done to prevent further juvenile violence. Despite the small numbers and percentages of these events, the media consistently represents them as "on the rise" and a growing problem. In reality, there is neither a rising nor a continuing trend. In the five-year period between 1992-93 and 1996-97, for example, there were an average of 26.8 gun murders per year on K-12 and university school property. In contrast, during the last five school years, 2009-10 to 2013-14, the average was 12—a 55 percent drop. This came despite the substantial increase in the overall number of students.

What has changed over time is the treatment of the mass murders as major media events. After each of the horrific incidents, media outlets flooded the public with images of the shootings. In 1999, the Columbine High School mass murders topped the list of crime stories covered during evening broadcasts for ABC, NBC, and

CBS with more than 319 stories—more than five times the total of any other incident. In the year following the massacre at Columbine High School, the nation's fifty largest newspapers printed nearly 10,000 stories related to the event and its aftermath, averaging one story per newspaper every other day. The coverage of the Virginia Tech incident was estimated at its peak to have more than 600 reporters on the scene and four or five acres of satellite television trucks. Realistically, there is no trend toward young and younger juvenile killings, and children are more likely to be killed by adults.

In essence, mass murders sell papers and attract viewers and listeners. In fact, school violence has also created a new industry developed around the issue of school safety. Technological solutions, equipment, grief counseling, and consulting on school safety plans have emerged. Ironically, certain political groups have appropriated the narrative of school shootings as a primary argument in favor of gun control. Others have pointed out that "Gun-Free Zones" can quickly become the killing fields of the unbalanced, who can act without fear of armed intervention.

Two cases are particularly relevant as illustrations of school mass murder and the subsequent media coverage that they generated—the Columbine High School and the Virginia Tech University mass killings. How the media presented these occurrences as major events, how they fit the criteria of a moral panic, and how they characterized the socio-psychological relationship of the perpetrators to the public established a pattern that continues in similar cases.

The evolution of the "juvenile delinquent"

In the post-World War II period, law enforcement authorities became aware of a previously under-reported phenomenon—an apparent increase in the incidence of crimes perpetrated by "teenagers." Dubbed "juvenile delinquency," it quickly became a subject of popular discussion, psychological study, and even entertainment in the form of movies such as "Blackboard Jungle" (1955), "High School Confidential" (1958), and in the Broadway hit musical and later movie, "West Side Story" (1956). Although previously referenced in such sociological studies as "Street Corner Society," its emergence as a media phenomenon was largely due to its capture of the public's attention. The search for causative factors cited such influences as "horror" comics, broken homes, the bad influence of the then-new television, rock 'n' roll music, and other media vehicles which tended to "glorify crime and/or criminals." Child and adolescent psychologists referenced the "alienated adolescent," and sympathetic depictions by actors such as Marlon Brando in "The Wild One" and James Dean in "Rebel Without a Cause" were exceptionally popular with the younger set.

Not surprisingly, the rebellious component apparent in juvenile delinquents (or "JD"s as they became known) attracted many young people. The interaction between the streets and the media resulted in a highly distinctive image, drawing components from various social—and antisocial—sources. Many of the traits that differentiated the delinquent from the average "clean-cut" young person paved the way for the visual and psychological delineation of what would be called the adolescent anti-social personality.

By the late '50s, the JD stereotype had become readily recognizable. He wore his hair longer and in more complex and flamboyant styles, such as the DA ("Duck's Ass"—the antithesis of the crew cut or short styles favored by the older generation). With the advent of rock 'n' roll music and Elvis Presley, sideburns were frequently part of the style.

Clothing consisted of jeans or black "pegged pants" and a tee shirt. A pack of cigarettes was often carried in a rolled-up sleeve. Headgear generally consisted of a peaked "motorcycle cap," and the favorite footwear was a short heavy boot with a pointed toe. The most emblematic feature of the "wardrobe" was invariably a black leather jacket frequently studded with metal, often emblazoned with a gang symbol. Preferred vehicles included motorcycles and hotrods.

Some of the most serious violence involving juvenile delinquents occurred in the conflicts between teenage gangs that could be based on race, territory, sexual rivalry, or perceived slights by others. Weaponry included switchblade knives, zip guns (firearms constructed from a cap gun and automobile antenna and designed to fire .22 caliber bullets), clubs, and tire chains. Traditional crimes associated with juvenile delinquents involved the turf wars of teenage gangs, robbery, assault, and multiple automobile-related infractions. This was to evolve dramatically with the later advent of drugs and computer-based technology.

The Columbine Mass Murders—The Time and the Place

To understand the evolution of the Columbine perpetrators, it is necessary to consider the changes that occurred in the socialization of children from the post-War period to the time of the crime. Traditionally, children's play had been largely gender-based. Girls played with dolls (pretending to be mothers or, with the advent with such fashion dolls as Barbie, acting the part of young adults). Boys typically engaged in such games as cowboys and badmen (or Indians) or soldiers, which was not surprising considering the number of fathers who had seen service in World War II.

Early children's television programs consisted of a large number of western-based shows, including *Roy Rogers*, *The Lone Ranger*, *Hopalong Cassidy*, and others. The popularity of the Western was also evidenced on prime-time TV through a series of Adult Westerns, some of which (*Wyatt Earp*, *Bat Masterson*) were based on actual historical characters, while others were fictional creations. In both the children's shows and the primetime presentations alike, moral values were heavily stressed. The TV show "Bonanza" garnered a global audience through its depiction of a close-knit family on the Nevada frontier.

Much of this was to change in the period starting in the late 1960s. A general disillusion with the Vietnam War resulted in the decreasing popularity of military-style toys and games. The women's movement brought about criticism of gender-based play, and the Native American movement roundly condemned the depiction of "Indians" as violent savages—even to the point of launching crusades against traditional college and high school team mascots, one of which had reached the major-league Washington Redskins by 2014. Guns came under pressure, and many parents refused to permit their children to own toy firearms or other weapons.

Ironically, even as the crusades against traditional toys and play formats were accelerating, new recreational and entertainment forms were emerging that would take both violence and sexuality to another level. These would include role-playing games, video games, and the emergence of the Super Hero. The video game was especially significant for several reasons. Players could now engage in solitary play without the need for others. Many games pitted the player against an opposing force that would ultimately destroy him. The exceptionally popular "Space Invaders" required the player to shoot and destroy alien figures that approached at an ever-faster rate. Though ultimately the player would "die," his or her success was measured in the number of aliens that were destroyed before the inevitable. Of course, a push of the "Reset" button brought the player back to life for another go.

As video games evolved with increasing technology, the violence escalated. More powerful gaming systems and increasingly realistic graphics proved most popular in games in which the player assumed an "anti-hero" or even criminal status. The exceptionally popular "Grand Theft Auto" (which was re-introduced several times with increasingly realistic formats) involved the killing of police and the murder of prostitutes.

Although certain parents' groups and others protested the more extreme video games and succeeded in having some of them rated (as movies are), many parents, lacking the computer involvement and skills of their children, were and are largely unaware of their content. Ironically, as technology has progressed, the games have become integrated into the communications media in such a way that the two are inseparable. They can now be accessed not only through specialized game boxes but directly on the same computer through which users receive the Internet, and on cell phones and other portable electronic devices. In this, some might be tempted to see a fixation with the games to the point of obsession.

However, video games as a cause of youth violence have become what some experts call "the latest scapegoat for violence." When the public is experiencing a "moral panic," they, and the media, frantically search for causes on which to pin blame. Marilyn Manson and other rockers and computers and video games have all been cited by an aging generation of authority figures, claims makers, and moral entrepreneurs who found themselves out of the loop due to widespread use of communications systems, much as an earlier generation blamed comics and rock music.

Thus, to what extent the entertainment media influenced the Columbine killers is impossible to judge, although it is tempting to surmise that in their costumes and plans for indiscriminate killing, Harris and Klebold saw themselves in the mold of super anti-heroes wreaking vengeance on an unjust society. Unfortunately, life offers no "Reset" button, and once the game was over, neither they nor their victims could be brought back.

The Columbine Case

On April 20, 1999, almost eight years to the date of the Oklahoma City Bombing, two high school seniors, Eric Harris and Dylan Klebold, shot and killed twelve students and one teacher and injured 21 other students at Columbine High School in Littleton, Colorado. After the mass murder, the pair committed suicide.

Harris, a talented student, was calm and calculating but had no real plans for his future. Klebold was more high strung and emotional with hopes of becoming a computer engineer. He had already been accepted by several colleges. Although the teens were bullied, they also bullied younger boys. They viewed themselves as "badasses" and outlaws. Just as adolescence is a time of rebellion and experimentation, it is also a time for trying on new identities and appearances.

Harris and Klebold were rumored to be "anti-jock." Students at Columbine High School, like most high schools, developed a social structure with types that included "geeks" or "nerds," "jocks," and "preppies." Subcultures whose norms and values ran counter to the popular culture were also represented. Whereas in the 1960s and 1970s these nonconformists were "greasers," "juvies," or "hippies," some of the present antisocial types took a darker turn and were referred to as "stoners," "Goths," or the "trench coat mafia."

Harris and Klebold associated themselves with the Trench Coat Mafia (TCM). Harris maintained a TCM webpage on AOL on which he ranted hateful diatribes largely directed against his classmates. The TCM exemplified the Goth or punk culture by wearing black, listening to heavy metal or death metal music, and worshiping Wicca or Satan. The connection of Harris and Klebold with the TCM was sensationalized in the press with images of psychopaths wearing long trench coats and spewing hate over the Internet, while plotting acts of senseless violence.

As at most high schools, the "jocks" were the dominant and popular group at Columbine. The school had a strong sports program, especially in football. Team members and associated coaches and cheerleaders were at the top of the social pyramid, a status resented by Harris and Klebold. They considered themselves to be fearsome, paramilitary figures. The pair spent many hours playing computer games, such as *Doom* and *Quake*, that are based upon first-person shooters and glorify combat. The reality involved more than games and play-acting. Harris was seething with rage and anger against authority and symbols of authority and had a suicidal ideation. He was diagnosed as obsessive-compulsive and was prescribed various psychotropic drugs. Klebold validated these feelings for Harris. Together, the boys were a dangerous combination.

Harris and Klebold had several encounters with the police. They stole items from school and other students, including a laptop. One incident involved property damage to a van parked in a parking lot and the theft of $400 worth of electrical equipment. They were sentenced to a juvenile diversion program since it was their first official (and a nonviolent) offense.

Prior to the massacre, the teens recorded tapes in their basements about their plans to attack their school. The tapes show them holding weapons and drinking from bottles of whiskey. One quote from Klebold on the tapes illustrates their attitudes:

> I hope we kill 250 of you. It will be the most nerve-wracking fifteen minutes of my life, after the bombs are set and we're waiting to charge through the school. Seconds will be like hours. I can't wait. I'll be shaking like a leaf. (Fast, 2008, 201).

Harris agrees, saying it's going to be like *Doom* (the video game) with no "target" left alive. The teens even fantasized on their tapes about a movie being made about their story with Quentin Tarantino as the director.

Both boys worked at a local pizza restaurant, which provided them with the money to purchase the guns, fireworks, ammunition, and propane tanks for their arsenal. Because neither boy was 18 at the time, they enlisted older co-workers and friends to buy guns at an area gun show. After one such transaction, Harris wrote in his diary:

> We . . . have . . . GUNS! We F***ing got em, you sons of bitches! HA! HA HA HA HA! Neener. Booga. Booga. Heh, it's all over now. This caps it off, the point of no return. . . . (Fast, 2008, 198).

They spent months planning, testing pipe bombs, and practicing shooting their weapons. The day of the actual shooting they had loaded their cars full of explosives, 20 gallons of gasoline, and an assortment of pipe bombs. For whatever reason, the bombs, some of which were placed beneath the athletes' usual lunch tables, did not detonate.

When their apocalyptic plans to blow up their school failed, Harris and Klebold decided to proceed anyway. Dressed in long, black coats with backpacks filled with pipe bombs and utility belts stuffed with shotgun shells, each teen carried a sawed-off shotgun. Harris also carried a Hi-Point 9mm carbine rifle. Klebold had a TEC semiautomatic handgun. Before they reached the entrance to the school, they fatally shot two students and wounded five others. One student, a friend of theirs, however, was warned not to enter the school.

At about 11:15 a.m., they entered the school and began to shoot seemingly at random any students they encountered. Despite their recorded disdain, specific individuals or types of students (i.e. jocks) were not targeted in the shootings; instead the objective seemed to be a high body count.

Harris and Klebold were heard laughing as students screamed in terror. Harris found a student hiding under a table and aimed his gun at her. He asked her if she believed in God. She replied, "Yes, I believe in God." Harris asked her why and then shot her to death. They reveled in their power to decide who lived and who died. According to two reporters who viewed the Columbine shooters' tapes, they wanted to be martyrs immortalized on film. Specifically, they wanted the notoriety of being the worst mass murderers in history.

Ultimately, the boys' obsession with "media immortality" would be realized. Multiple media outlets quickly appeared, and the Columbine mass murders dominated the airwaves, with CNN broadcasting it all day long. Considering the short attention span of the media, the reportage lasted for an unusually long time, a full month. According to one later account:

> The cameras offered the illusion we were witnessing the event. But the cameras had arrived too late. Eric and Dylan had retreated inside after five minutes. The cameras missed the outside murders and could not follow Eric and Dylan inside. The fundamental experience for most of America was *almost* witnessing mass murder. It was

the panic and frustration of not knowing, the mounting terror of horror withheld, just out of view. (Cullen, 2009, 66)

After the shootings, forums were developed to debate issues surrounding the massacre. A common theme was whether Harris and Klebold should be forgiven, with most individuals feeling sympathy or empathy for the pair. Curiously—especially given the pair's alienation from the student body and complaints of bullying—when the students erected a series of memorial crosses for those who had died, they included two for the killers.

The Virginia Tech Shootings—The Time and the Place
In a truly free society, freedom of speech and personal expression are among the most highly valued and jealously guarded privileges. In the United States, the civil liberties defined by the Bill of Rights have been reaffirmed by the courts, even as they have been invoked by groups and movements considered by the vast majority of citizens to be un-American. Nazi sympathizers, Communists, and anti-military protestors have paradoxically sought refuge behind the foundation stones of a government that represents that which they wish to change or destroy.

Though not specifically enumerated in the Constitution, the concept of privacy rights has more recently become a legislative issue, as electronic and communications technology have facilitated both government and commercial intrusion into the private sphere. Unfortunately, just as our governmental system protects socially unpopular persons and causes, it can also provide a situation that aids the deranged individual in the commission of tragic and horrifying acts. This came into especially high relief in the media following the shootings of Monday, April 16, 2007, on the campus of the Virginia Polytechnic Institute and State University (Virginia Tech).

As with the Columbine shootings, a heightened level of concern surrounded the rampage and its impact on society. Many of the questions following the Virginia Tech massacre had to do with whether or not the incident could have been prevented through intervention prior to the event. In effect, was the shooter, Seung-Hui Cho, exhibiting signs that, if correctly interpreted, might have called for intervention and, if so, how? Also, was Cho's ability to buy firearms a contributing factor? Equally important, did the prohibition against legally carried firearms facilitate the massacre?

As an institution with a long heritage of education in fields such as engineering, technology, and science, Virginia Tech seemed a highly improbable locale for the events that transpired there. Unlike schools with a historically high involvement in socio-political causes and events, students involved in a more "vocational" curriculum tend to be more focused on their field. Further, the university maintained reasonable security protocols (including key-card-only access to residence halls) and a zero-tolerance policy for firearms on campus.

In the aftermath of the disaster, a special panel was appointed to evaluate the situation, and there was extensive discussion in the media. Perhaps the most constructive outcome was a series of improvements in the National Instant Criminal Background Check System (NICS) to screen gun purchases and preclude criminals, the mentally ill, and certain others, from purchasing firearms through conventional channels. After all of the comment, study, and discussion though, the questions remained. Is an individual's bizarre behavior, in the absence of real harm to himself or others, cause for legal intervention? To what extent are an individual's medical records regarding mental state and conditions subject to privacy protections? And, if they can be accessed, who should have that authority and under what circumstances? Had Cho not been able to purchase firearms through a retail outlet, would he have procured them by theft or through illegal means? As mentioned, did the zero-tolerance policy for guns on campus deprive responsible individuals of personal protection and thereby contribute to the death toll?

These questions, of course, are still being debated. The reality is that laws and regulations lose their meaning and effectiveness in the mind of the deranged individual. Cho represented himself with a question mark. Despite the best efforts of observers, authorities, academics, and medical practitioners, that is what he remains.

The Virginia Tech Case

On April 16, 2007, a 23-year-old, full-time student at Virginia Polytechnic Institute (Virginia Tech), Seung-Hui Cho, killed a total of 32 students and faculty and wounded 25 others before taking his own life. Virginia Tech is located in Blacksburg, Virginia, a rural, quiet college town with very little crime.

Cho had a lifelong history of severe social impairment and a history of mental illness. At a very young age, Cho, with his sister and parents, emigrated from Korea to the United States. They lived for a short period in Chicago before moving to a northern Virginia suburb. Cho's parents opened a dry cleaning business and worked long hours so that Cho and his sister could attend the best schools. As a result, Cho received very little attention from his parents, who were always working and reportedly not warm or communicative. Some accounts maintained that Cho was poked fun at in high school because of his heavily accented speech. When he would read in school, students would laugh and say, "go home to China."

Cho received special education in high school including language and art therapy. His teachers and his art therapist were disturbed by his withdrawn behaviors and his writings, which included an expressed desire "to repeat Columbine." The school instructed Cho's parents to arrange for a psychiatric evaluation, after which he was diagnosed with severe depression and selective mutism. Even his own family was unable to communicate with him.

The signs of being a troubled young man were exhibited long before the shootings took place at Virginia Tech. Cho was socially isolated—a self-imposed isolation, since he would not talk or communicate with other students. When asked a question, he would typically look down, look away, respond only after twenty to thirty seconds had passed and then reply in a barely audible whisper. Very much aware of his "invisibility," he adopted an identity, "question mark," which he used on Facebook.

During his junior year in 2005, Cho enrolled in a writing class taught by well-known poet Nikki Giovanni. The poet became disturbed about the images of death and the bizarre references in Cho's poems. She finally had Cho removed from her class stating that he was "mean." One of the directors of the writing program at Virginia Tech, Lucinda Roy, then began tutoring Cho herself. She remembered how he hid his face with sunglasses and a cap. She recommended to Cho that he go to the University's counseling program but he refused.

Cho was also accused of stalking two female students at the school in his junior year. The local police warned Cho about his behavior after one of the women reported him. Upset by the women's complaint, he sent an instant message to his suitemate saying, "I might as well kill myself." His suitemate contacted campus police, and Cho was referred to a mental health clinic at Carilion St. Albans Behavioral Health Center for assessment. Cho kept secret his prior counseling and pharmacologic treatment (paroxitime-20mg., which he was prescribed for almost a year) during his assessment. He was ordered to receive treatment at Virginia Tech Cook Counseling Center, and in the presence of the Health Center staff he made an appointment by telephone. He never kept his appointment, and there was no follow-up since he was a voluntary patient.

In February, 2007, Cho was able to purchase a handgun over the Internet that was delivered to a pawn store. The background check apparently did not pick up his mental health visit. He was able to purchase a semi-automatic pistol the next month. During his final weeks, Cho became totally immersed in planning his rampage, practicing shooting guns at a shooting range, and recording a video.

Cho's killing spree began at about 7:00 a.m. at the West Ambler Johnston Residence Hall where he shot and killed two people. The University Police, alerted by reports of gunshots, arrived at the residence hall. Believing it to be an isolated incident, the University Police failed to alert the student body for another few hours. The local Blacksburg police were led to believe by Virginia Tech administrators that the situation was "domestic" in nature and so they focused their efforts on the boyfriend (known to be a gun owner) of a young victim, Emily Hilscher. They suspected the boyfriend had killed Hilscher in an angry fight, and the young man was kept in custody for several hours.

In the meantime, Cho returned to his own residence hall and changed his bloody clothes. He then blended with the crowd and managed to take a trip to the post office where he mailed a set of writings and videotapes to the NBC network. He next entered Norris Hall, an engineering and mathematics building, carrying two semi-automatic handguns with about 400 rounds of ammunition, a hammer and a knife. Afterward, he chained the main doors from the inside and climbed the stairs to the second floor. He then began entering classrooms, walking down the aisles and systematically and silently shooting anyone he encountered. A survivor, Trey Perkins, stated that Cho never said a word and that he never saw a straighter face.

The DVD produced by Cho shows video clips of him staring aggressively at the camera, tightly holding guns in both hands and wearing a backwards black baseball cap, fingerless black gloves, and a black T-shirt under a khaki vest. Similar to the Columbine shooters, Cho wore paramilitary clothing. Also similar to the Columbine shooting, a video was made providing the shooter with a platform to vent his rage and frustration with the world. He also praised "Eric and Dylan" and referred to them as "martyrs." Although there was no evidence of Cho being bullied at Virginia Tech, his writings and tapes expressed contempt for his fellow students as privileged, spoiled, and morally corrupted by a materialistic society. One excerpt from his videotape is as follows:

> You never felt an ounce of pain. Your Mercedes weren't enough, you brats. Your golden chains weren't enough, you snobs. Your trust fund wasn't enough, your drunken debaucheries weren't enough. You drove me to do this. (Davies, 2007, 18)

One authority on the case asserts that the shootings were an attempt by Cho to act out his violent fantasies and to create a media spectacle with Cho as the director and star.

Newer forms of the media communicated news about the shooting, as did the traditional news outlets. Students from Virginia Tech disseminated cell phone images of the event, as well as commentary on Facebook, YouTube and their own media spaces. After the shootings, a digitized memory bank was also created to share grief and discuss the event on a website. In effect, the new media provided a way for individuals to collectively mourn and to try to make sense out of the senseless.

The administration and campus police at Virginia Tech were widely criticized for their failure to alert students immediately after the shootings at Johnston Residence Hall. It was argued that had they quickly called off classes they could have prevented the deadliest school shooting in the United States. In 2012, the school was found negligent in a lawsuit filed by two families of slain students.

Several hypotheses have been advanced to explain these school mass murders, including the influence of media violence, school bullying, mental illness of the perpetrator(s), easy ability to buy guns, and a culture of violence. In reality, school violence is multi-faceted and could be caused by any or all of these factors. Certainly, more research is needed to understand the dynamics of such tragedies.

In the age of "instant communication," cell phone pictures, texting, posting on YouTube and Facebook have become prominent news media and conveyors of information, with the newer forms of the media capturing news as it happens or earlier than the more traditional forms. A virtual hysteria is created to get the story first and distribute the information as fast as possible.

However, despite the media narration of increasing violent crime, there is no evidence to support that American society is under siege by a tidal wave of youthful super predators. As previously cited, there is also no evidence that school fatalities are increasing. In fact, school mass murders are rare. Despite the extensive media coverage accorded both the Columbine and Virginia Tech incidents, the moral panic over mass murders in the school environment is disproportionate to the nature of the threat and greater than empirical evidence justifies.

There are similarities that exist in both the Columbine and Virginia Tech cases. In both instances, the perpetrators did not "snap" but instead carefully planned and orchestrated the events. Cho, like Harris and Klebold, spent months planning, obtaining weapons, practicing using those weapons, and making videotapes. Also similar is the claim that Harris and Klebold and Cho were bullied or at least they perceived themselves to be marginalized in their school environment. Certainly their videos provide ample evidence of their anger toward their classmates based on what their classmates "did to them."

Finally, the shooters utilized electronic media to record the perceived reasons for their rage and their plans. Knowing that electronic postings would reach millions and that, following their acts, the conventional media would have access to their diatribes—and, in all likelihood, broadcast them to millions more—raises the disquieting probability that all or some part of their actions were motivated by, as has been stated of Cho, the "desire to stage a media event." The perpetrators of the school violence wanted to leave an electronic testimonial of their actions.

Although in the past criminals have used the conventional media—primarily newspapers—for personal gratification or as a means of publicizing manifestos and demands, various personal electronic media have provided the means of reaching a wide audience, both at present and into the future, and achieving what might be called "Internet immortality." In 1964, communications theorist, Marshall McCluhan, defined the difference between what he referred to as "cool" media and "hot" media and, in the process, predicted the Internet. His belief was that "electronic interdependence" would result in a collective identity that he referred to as the "global village." As Columbine and Virginia Tech demonstrates, it can alternatively become a part of a horrific demonstration of anger and alienation.

Chapter 6
Celebrity Cases: Beautiful People—Ugly Deeds

On June 17, 1989, Americans watched their televisions in disbelief as a live feed from helicopters in Los Angeles showed police engaged in the low-speed chase of a white Ford Bronco carrying football legend and movie star, O.J. Simpson. From the start, the arrest and trial of Simpson for the murder of his ex-wife, Nicole, and her friend, Ronald Goldman, would be a media event in which all players–including the defendant, the prosecutor, the witnesses, the judge, and the "Dream Team" of defense attorneys–would interact with the cameras as much or more than with each other. It would become, perhaps, the most blatant example of the symbiosis between the media and the justice system in the 20th century. It has been referred to as the "Trial of the Century," less in terms of hyperbole and more in terms of spectacle.

O.J. Simpson—The Time and the Place

"Image" has always been an important component of celebrity, and perhaps nowhere has image been more carefully cultivated than in the realms of sports and entertainment. When several major scandals occurred in the early days of Hollywood (the most notable of which involved sex/murder accusations against silent film star, Roscoe "Fatty" Arbuckle), studios insisted that "morals clauses" be inserted into the contracts of stars and carefully monitored their behavior. Studio security departments befriended reporters and major media figures and insured that any bad behavior was kept from the public. When Hollywood screen goddess Jean Harlow's husband, Paul Bern, died under suspicious circumstances, studio personnel arrived well in advance of the authorities.

Sports figures likewise carefully cultivated the media and secured their cooperation through interviews and access. This was not particularly difficult, since media figures justified their sanitized portrayals as preserving the reputations of stars who set an example for their young fans. Only years later would sports fans learn about the drinking and womanizing proclivities of stars such as Babe Ruth and Mickey Mantle. When celebrities ran afoul of the morals clause or the law, the public looked on in fascination.

The post-Watergate era, with its emphasis on investigative reporting in venues ranging from politics to business to entertainment, brought about a new cynicism. A public that once stood aghast at celebrity antics, now smugly sought to discover how much could be gotten away with. Revelations such as presidential infidelities, addictions, and "kinky" sexual practices left the public jaded. Only a major scandal involving truly significant characters engaged in the worst possible behavior could capture their attention. The O.J. Simpson case would succeed on all counts.

The O.J. Simpson Case

Orenthal James "O.J." Simpson was more than a major sports figure. He was a public persona of iconic proportions. Considered by many to be the greatest running back in the history of the NFL, his good looks and affability made him an interviewer's, and a publicist's, delight. Even before closing out his Hall of Fame sports career, he had been tapped for parts in films and television. He also appeared in advertisements and commercials for a number of companies, most notably a very popular series produced for Hertz Rent-a-Car. Simpson also retained his connection with football through stints as a commentator and through interviews.

Twice married and divorced, Simpson had three children by his first marriage (one of whom died at age 2 in a drowning accident) and two with his second wife, Nicole Brown. Despite a stormy marriage that resulted in a domestic violence charge (1989) to which Simpson pleaded "No Contest," following their 1991 divorce, he and Nicole were seen together at events involving their children and were rumored to have maintained a personal relationship.

On June 13, 1994, at 12:00 a.m., Nicole and her friend, Ron Goldman, were found murdered outside Brown's condominium. The killing was exceptionally vicious, Nicole having been stabbed multiple times in the throat. Detectives arriving at the scene noted a number of objects, including a knit cap, keys, an envelope, and a bloodstained left-hand glove. When they discovered the identity of the victim—and the fact that her children aged 6 and 9 were asleep upstairs in the condo—two of the detectives were sent to contact Simpson regarding their care, even though, as a family member, he would be considered a suspect in the case.

Upon arriving at Simpson's residence, Detectives Fuhrman and Lange discovered a white Ford Bronco with an apparent blood spot near the driver's door handle. Though lights were plainly visible inside the main house, several telephone calls went unanswered. When there was no response at the front door, they proceeded to inquire at the three bungalows on the property. One of the bungalows housed Arnelle Simpson, O.J.'s oldest daughter. She accompanied several detectives to the main house, which they entered and found empty. Fuhrman then interviewed the resident of the first bungalow, a self-described friend and houseguest named Kato Kaelin. Kaelin confirmed that on the previous evening, Simpson had left on a trip to Chicago. Contacted by phone at his Chicago hotel, Simpson sounded distraught and promised to catch the next available flight home.

Returning to the main house from Kato Kaelin's bungalow, Detective Fuhrman discovered a bloodstained right-hand leather glove along the walkway. A further inspection of the Ford Bronco revealed more apparent blood drops, as well as a trail leading to the front door. Criminalists were contacted to examine and catalog the scene and to seize the Bronco for inspection. By the early morning, police were preparing a search warrant for Simpson's property and had established him as a probable suspect in the case.

An autopsy that morning confirmed the brutality of the crime, as well as the strength of the attacker. The slash wound across Nicole's neck came close to decapitating her. Observations indicated that both Goldman and Nicole had been attacked from behind. The weapon appeared to be a knife with an approximately 6-inch blade, such as one Simpson had recently purchased. Following the autopsy, blood samples were obtained for analysis and comparison with the blood at the crime scene. The DNA portion of the testing would be done by an independent laboratory. Blood samples, as well as the evidence and photographs gathered by police at the Simpson home, would later figure prominently in the defense's alternative theories about the case.

Ongoing police interviews resulted in the identification of two important witnesses: Allan Park, the driver who chauffeured Simpson to the airport, arrived 20 minutes earlier than the suggested 10:45 p.m. time. Unable to reach anyone inside the house, he saw a man crossing the grounds to the doorway at 10:50 p.m. When he tried the phone again, he reached O.J. Simpson who claimed to have overslept but who, he noted, was sweating heavily. Jill Shively, who lived near Nicole, claimed to have seen O.J. Simpson driving at a high speed and running a red light at approximately 11:00 p.m. (Shively's appearance for money on an interview show resulted in her elimination as a witness.)

When DNA tests on the glove from the crime scene confirmed the blood as belonging to Simpson and both victims, an arrest warrant was issued, and Simpson's attorney, Robert Shapiro, was contacted. Because of his celebrity status, it was arranged that Simpson, who was at the home of his friend, Robert Kardashian, would surrender at 11:00 a.m. When he failed to appear, police proceeded to his last-known location. Since shortly after the discovery of the crime and the identification of the victims, the media had marshaled extensive resources to report from on-site. Simpson's estate was surrounded, as was the crime scene, and police and anyone suspected of involvement in or knowledge of the case was consistently badgered. When, at a 2:00 p.m. press conference it was announced that Simpson had been named in a warrant and was sought as a fugitive, they were handed the opportunity of a lifetime.

The drama continued several hours later when Simpson's attorney made a televised appeal for Simpson to surrender and then read a message from Simpson that sounded very much like a suicide note. Almost two hours later, by tracing cell phone calls, it was confirmed that Simpson and his friend, Al Cowlings, were in Orange County and on the run.

Once the white Ford Bronco had been spotted, police began to close in. Cowlings telephoned that Simpson was suicidal and holding a gun to his head, and there began a low-speed chase, followed by helicopters from area television stations as well as the police. In a short time, the television networks had preempted local programming throughout the United States in favor of live coverage of the pursuit. Shortly before 8:00 p.m. (Pacific Time), the Bronco drove past the media gauntlet and into Simpson's estate, where, after some negotiations, he surrendered.

On June 17th, Simpson and his friend, Al Cowlings, were processed at police headquarters. Two days later, Simpson was to plead "not guilty." At the time of his arraignment, Judge Lance Ito was appointed to hear the case. Of Japanese-American ancestry, Ito had a reputation for eccentric, and sometimes emotional, behavior. It was rumored that Ito had been appointed because, as an Asian-American, he would not be viewed as either "White" or "Black," an important consideration in a trial that was expected to excite racial tensions.

Simpson's lead attorney, Robert Shapiro, was experienced in handling high-profile clients. Keenly aware of the publicity that would be generated by the trial, he assembled a defense team that included some of the most noted criminal law practitioners of the time, including F. Lee Bailey, Alan Dershowitz and Johnny Cochran. The group would be referred to in the media as the "Dream Team"—a reference to the American gold medal Olympic basketball team. Ironically, despite their high-powered reputations, several of the top names were inexperienced in murder trials, though accomplished in self-promotion and publicity.

Heading the prosecution team was Marcia Clark, age 41, a California native and veteran prosecutor. A rape victim and veteran of an abusive marriage at the time of the Simpson case, she was involved in a bitter custody dispute—circumstances that many felt colored her approach. When she appeared in the courtroom wearing an "angel pin" identical to pins worn by members of the Brown family, defense objected, and she was instructed to remove the pin. Her primary assistant through most of the trial was career prosecutor, Christopher Darden—like Simpson, an African American.

In the opinion of many observers, neither the prosecution nor the defense represented the best of the legal system. The decision by the Los Angeles District Attorney to move the trial from Santa Monica—where the crimes took place—to downtown Los Angeles would have a far-reaching impact on the makeup of the jury and the strategies of both the prosecution and the defense.

Mindful of the riots that occurred in the aftermath of the Rodney King case, the D.A. feared that if a predominantly white jury was impaneled in Santa Monica and subsequently convicted Simpson, racial tensions would again ignite. The jury that finally was selected was composed of one Hispanic, one white, eight African Americans, and two of mixed descent. An alternate jury included one Hispanic, four white people, and several African Americans.

The trial was to be the culmination of the media circus that had begun at the crime scene, continued through the pursuit, and simmered for the months preceding the trial. In addition to the daily coverage provided by the international gathering of newspaper and TV reporters, the case, and peripheral aspects of it, were discussed at length in news magazines, entertainment tabloids, fan and lifestyle magazines, and on radio and television interview shows, and news magazine formats. Media from around the world provided daily coverage.

From early on, it became clear that the positions taken by both the prosecution and defense were calculated to appeal to their larger audience, as much as to the jury. The prosecution attempted to paint Simpson as a violent and abusive spouse by presenting a history of domestic violence during the couple's 17-year relationship and who was ultimately unable to cope with the fact that his wife divorced him and, therefore, pursued her in a jealous rage. Goldman became a victim when he showed up at the wrong place and time to return a pair of sunglasses.

The defense characterized Simpson as an innocent black man, who, in addition to being purposely framed by the system, was the victim of sloppy police practices on the part of officers, criminalists, and analysts responsible for handling the evidence. As early as the opening statements, Marcia Clark referenced the "trail of blood" as "devastating proof of his guilt." African American Johnny Cochran countered with quotes from Martin Luther King, accusations of a "rush to judgment," and, in a later statement, that the evidence in the case was "contaminated, compromised, and ultimately corrupted." The defense team essentially put the LAPD on trial. Cochran also, in a less-than-subtle manner, reminded the black jurors of what might happen if they were to convict Simpson. The courtroom coverage was largely focused on the dynamics of the legal actors and how well they were playing to the public. The reality of the special treatment accorded Simpson was ignored, as was the fact that the Simpson trial was a far cry from the criminal justice experience of most defendants.

The trial, which began on January 23, 1995, would continue into early October. Both sides wandered off-point with bizarre alternative theories. The defense suggested that Nicole and Goldman had something to do with cocaine and might have been killed by drug dealers. Another foray involved characterizing Detective Mark Fuhrman as a racist. Judge Ito's rulings throughout were frequently inconsistent and difficult to fathom—as when he permitted the defense to ask Fuhrman whether he had used the word "Nigger" at any time within the past decade. Ultimately, as some alleged, Cochran played the "race card" to the hilt and referred to Fuhrman as a "lying genocidal racist cop."

In the course of the coverage, the mass media did everything possible to "hook" the public by turning the coverage into an ongoing soap opera. Noted journalists, attorneys, crime writers, and others provided daily coverage in the form of broadcasts and articles that combined reportage on trial events with speculation on the eventual outcome. The fact that the primary participants in the proceedings played to the audience, as well as the jury, heightened the entertainment value. Adding to the dramatic tension, especially among white residents of the Los Angeles community, was the very real fear that, as with the Rodney King verdict, the jury's decision might possibly provoke race riots.

Because the strongest aspect of the prosecution's case linking Simpson to the murders involved the identification of blood evidence at various locations, it became necessary to familiarize the jury with the scientific principles and processes involved. The result was an extended period of mind-numbing testimony by both expert witnesses and the criminalists and lab workers involved in processing the evidence. Despite the fact that the lack of drama resulted in much of the public "tuning out" of this part of the case, the presence of the media may well have contributed to the self-protective stance adopted by many of the witnesses. Throughout this phase of the trial, the defense team attempted to sow doubt with a variety of theories ranging from careless handling of blood specimens to the planting of evidence as a part of a police conspiracy.

Of all the evidentiary exhibits, the ones that would form the most memorable impression, both during and after the trial, were the brown leather gloves, one of which was found at the crime scene and the other on the grounds of Simpson's home. After establishing the make and origin of the gloves, the prosecution insisted that Simpson try one of the gloves on. With his hands encased in latex gloves, Simpson appeared to have trouble putting the glove on. A representative from the gloves' manufacturer testified that the moisture had caused the gloves to shrink as much as a full size, and, in fact, when Simpson tried on a new pair of the same size, they fit perfectly. Defense attorney Johnny Cochran, however, saw the first attempt as key to an acquittal verdict and, referring to the glove, reminded the jury several times "if it doesn't fit, you must acquit."

In addition to the gloves, the prosecution linked bloody footprints at the murder site to an expensive and uncommon pair of designer shoes that Simpson denied owning. However, a photograph showed him wearing an identical pair. Fiber evidence in Goldman's shirt matched socks found at Simpson's bedroom, while other fiber samples linked the cap from the crime scene to the Ford Bronco and the glove from Simpson's premises. The defense would counter the blood evidence through the use of an expert witness who testified that a chemical (EDTA) commonly used in preserving laboratory blood specimens degraded the DNA in the sample and negated the prosecution's case.

Further incompetence on the part of the prosecution was demonstrated by the series of events they chose to ignore in presenting the case—preferring instead to stake virtually everything on the complexities of the blood evidence. These included the witness who had seen Simpson driving the Bronco near the murder site on the night of the murder; Simpson's purchase of a knife that could be the murder weapon; and a conversation overheard by a jail guard between Simpson and football star-turned-minister, Roosevelt Greer, in which Simpson yelled, "I didn't mean to do it. I'm sorry."

As the trial moved toward its conclusion, the media moved into high gear, albeit with distinctly racial overtones. In his study comparing racial perceptions and the effect of local (Los Angeles) media coverage on the trial, Dr. Darnell Hunt traces the trajectory of perception and coverage in both the local mass media and black media. Quoting an article by E.R. Shippe published in the *Columbia Journalism Review* three months prior to the trial, Shippe asks,

> Was he singled out for prosecution because of his preference for white women and because the murder victims were white? Have the mainstream media replaced the old lynch mob in destroying a black man perceived to have violated racial taboos? Is he the latest victim of a racist society's conspiracy to destroy black men? Can any black man, even one as wealthy as O.J., get a fair trial? (Shippe, 1994, 39)

As Dr. Hunt observes, "each of these concerns would figure prominently in the construction of the O.J. narrative circulated by the Los Angeles Sentinel" (the leading local black newspaper).

What was observed in Los Angeles was also being played out in cities across the country with large African American populations and, as the trial drew to its conclusion, police chiefs and local officials put police on alert. On Friday, September 29th, instructions were issued to the jury by Judge Ito with a proviso that they begin actual deliberation on Monday, October 2nd. After deliberating a little more than five hours, the jury announced a verdict. Judge Ito indicated that it would be read the following morning at 10:00 a.m.

The resultant "Not Guilty" verdict, while exultantly received by the black community, was met with skepticism and anger, not only in the white community but internationally. A British newspaper ran an extensive article on the trial under the headline, "What a Farce." Others questioned the integrity of the American justice system.

Bitter and angry as a result of the verdict, the families of Ronald Goldman and Nicole Brown proceeded with plans to institute a civil suit. A little more than a year later, in Santa Monica, the trial began with a jury of one black, one Hispanic, one Asian, and nine whites. Proceeding under different legal requirements, including the need to prove guilt by a preponderance of evidence rather than beyond a reasonable doubt, and the ability of the plaintiffs to call the defendant as a witness, the trial concluded with a favorable verdict of $8.5 million in damages to the Goldmans and $25 million between Nicole's children and Fred Goldman, father of Ron Goldman.

Now largely a pariah, Simpson would occasionally score news items by virtue of bizarre behavior and publicity seeking. A road rage incident in 2000, domestic disputes with his current girlfriend, occasional media appearances, and a 2007 book titled, "If I Did It," in which Simpson purportedly describes how he "would have" committed the murders, kept Simpson in the public consciousness, even while diminishing his popularity. In 2008, having been convicted of armed robbery, kidnapping, and assault for his part in the botched robbery of a sports memorabilia dealer, he was sentenced to 15 years in prison, where he remains as of 2015.

The media involvement in the Simpson trial and afterward proved to be significant on multiple levels. Although any jury trial requires a good degree of presentation on the part of both the prosecution and the defense, the extent of media coverage resulted in participants crossing the line from presentation to performance. To what degree this resulted in procedural and judgmental inadequacies on both sides is open to conjecture, but a number of factors are self-evident. The selection of a "Dream Team" of attorneys—better known for their flamboyant characters than their skill or experience in similar trials—certainly produced an effect. The ability of media exposure to launch a number of participants, including prosecutor, Marcia Clark, and witness, Mark Fuhrman, on second careers demonstrates the incentive of playing to the larger audience.

Whether the racial component would have had the same effect had the trial proceeded without the entertainment quotient is open to question. The fact that the jury chose to largely disregard what many whites felt was a preponderance of evidence certainly heightened tensions on both sides. Tragically, what was lost in the irrational arguments, the glare of celebrity, and the media spotlight is the fact that ultimately lives were lost, families damaged, and potential wasted. This was true for Nicole Brown Simpson, Ronald Goldman, and, ironically, for O.J. Simpson as well.

John Gotti, Jr.—The Time and the Place

The origins of organized crime in America can be traced back to the street gangs of the early to mid-19th century. Generally composed of immigrants, the gangs were frequently based on ethnicity and localized around a particular area or leader. Prior to the organization of the New York City Fire Department in 1865, politicians frequently sponsored volunteer companies that in turn supported their other activities—some of which were illegal.

Although street gang activity was and remains a significant problem in urban areas, no other group has ever achieved the levels of influence, wealth, efficiency and notoriety as has the Italian organization known variously as La Cosa Nostra or the Mafia. To understand the way in which their influence grew, as well as the traditions and skill sets that supported their success, it is necessary to consider their origins.

Since ancient times, the island of Sicily has been a battleground for powers ranging from the ancient Greeks to the Americans, English, and Germans in the Second World War. As a result, Sicilian peasants typically forged strong family loyalties and identified heavily with their particular towns or communities. A not-surprising outgrowth of this siege mentality was the formation of a number of secret societies, including the Black Hand and La Cosa Nostra. Characterized by stringent membership requirements, blood oaths, and elaborate initiation ceremonies, the societies showed no hesitation in victimizing their own countrymen.

Rampant poverty caused many Italians—especially those from the south of Italy—to seek a better life in America. Isolated by their language, they tended, like the earlier immigrant groups, to cluster in ethnic enclaves where their customs, foods, and mutual support provided a degree of comfort as they established themselves. It would not be long before career criminals and members of the secret societies would arrive to take advantage of the immigrants.

In 1892, Giuseppe Morello arrived in the United States. Initially involved in counterfeiting, Morello would go on to build the first Mafia family in America. In a short time, criminal activities would expand to extortion, gambling, prostitution, and murder for hire. As criminal activities increased and the media took notice of a number of sensational murder cases, the New York Police Department recognized that the difficulty of the problem was compounded by the fact that many Italian citizens who spoke no English could not communicate with the largely Irish police force. In 1905, Police Commissioner William McAdoo organized the Italian Squad—a select group of Italian-speaking police officers specifically assigned to address the growing problems in Little Italy (the lower New York community dominated by Italians). The man appointed to head the Squad was Officer (later Lieutenant) Joseph Petrosino. Courageous, intelligent, and possessed of a genius for investigation, Petrosino saw the problem not as a series of individual crimes but as a web of connected criminal activities extending into cities throughout the United States and back to Sicily. Realizing that much of the criminal element in America would have records back home, he established contacts with the police in Italy and, in 1909, received permission to travel to Italy to complete his investigation. While in Palermo, he was murdered.

The hierarchical nature of what was now known as the Mafia lent itself well to organization and specialization. A particularly lucrative area involved the sales of specialty vegetables, and a Mafia figure named Ciro Terranova proudly referred to himself as "The Artichoke King" even to the point of having artichokes embroidered on certain clothing items.

By the close of the First World War, Mafia families were well established in America's major cities. For the most part, they kept a low profile and retained their principal involvements inside the Italian community. In 1919, two events occurred that would forever change not only the Mafia but the history of crime in America—the Volstead Act, which authorized Prohibition effective January 1, 1920, was passed by Congress; and a young thug named Al Capone came west from Brooklyn to join his mentor, John Torrio, in Chicago.

By banning the sale of intoxicating beverages, the government unwittingly opened a world of opportunity for criminals. "Bootlegging"—whether in the form of manufacturing and distributing brewed and distilled liquors or of surreptitiously importing them from Europe, South America, and Canada—was intensely profitable. Moreover, in necessitating an elaborate network of supply chains and distribution channels, it resulted in heightened organizational skills that would provide the Mafia with ongoing involvement in legitimate businesses and trade unions. Because most people held Prohibition in contempt, the criminals who helped them obtain their supplies of spirits attained celebrity status and coverage in the media.

All this was not without its social cost. Bitter wars over territory on the part of different gangs resulted in shootings and bombings in which innocent people were killed. If there was a single act of violence that inspired widespread public revulsion with the criminal empires, it occurred on February 14, 1929, in Chicago, when gunmen in the employ of Al Capone gunned down seven members of rival George "Bugs" Moran's gang in what would be known as the St. Valentine's Day Massacre. The massacre is widely credited with making Al Capone a household name. Subsequently, agents from the Treasury Department were able to convict Capone on tax evasion charges and send him to prison.

The repeal of Prohibition in 1932 left the Mafia in an extremely strong position. Although occasional wars would erupt between the "families" over questions of leadership or territory, the Mob's financial resources enabled them to move into multiple legitimate businesses, and even to go international. In the '20s and '30s, they extended their control to include many of the resorts and casinos in Havana, Cuba, long a popular vacation destination. Following the War, Benjamin "Bugsy" Siegel, utilizing funds provided by gangsters, built the Flamingo—Las Vegas's first luxury resort. The Mafia's powerful Hollywood connections were instrumental in bringing top-flight entertainment that instantly popularized Las Vegas as a gambling Mecca.

The rise and increasing power of organized crime was facilitated by the fact that J. Edgar Hoover, head of the Federal Bureau of Investigation, for many years refused to acknowledge its existence and concentrated Bureau resources against bank robbers, spies, and Communists. Although criticized in the media for his intransigence, he remained steadfast until local police in the small town of Apalachin, New York, uncovered a "summit meeting" of organized crime figures from throughout the country in 1957. Over 60 underworld figures from multiple crime families were detained and later indicted. The conference undermined Hoover's contention that organized crime was merely a local problem to be handled by local police.

The Apalachin meeting was demonstrative of the Mafia's desire to remain as invisible as possible. Many believed that Al Capone's love of publicity and heavy media presence was a major factor in the government's movement against him. Except for the occasional sensational execution-style murders by errant members, most Mob bosses tended to keep a low profile.

Starting with the Kefauver hearings (United States Senate Special Committee to Investigate Crime) in 1950 and '51, the Federal government launched a number of efforts to attack the Mafia and its ancillary allies. It was the Kefauver Committee and its investigations that first put Mafia figures on national television. Television viewers were fascinated by Tennessee Senator Estes Kefauver and his questioning of Italian and Sicilian individuals about their illegal activities. Robert F. Kennedy was especially vigorous in exposing the union corruption fostered by Jimmy Hoffa who later disappeared and whose fate remains unknown. The Kefauver Committee findings have been criticized, as have the media, for sensationalizing a few gangsters who fit the Mafia image and for dramatizing organized crime more than investigating it.

As a fearsome and distinctive presence in American life for over a century, the Mafia and some of its more colorful characters have become legendary. From the multiple books and movies dealing with Capone's rise and fall to Francis Ford Coppola's "Godfather" trilogy, the well-heeled, immaculately dressed Mafia Don—complete with expensive automobile and eye-catching female companion—has become part of the folklore. John Gotti, Jr., exemplified this flashy mob persona and courted publicity with a sly smirk and a wink.

The John Gotti, Jr., Case

John Gotti, Jr., was the flamboyant, well-dressed "capo di tutti capi" (boss of all bosses) or "Godfather" of the New York Gambino organized crime family in the 1990s. He acted out his role in a highly visible way and became a darling of the media, featured in the pages of local and national tabloids. The media nicknamed him the "Dapper Don"—a tribute to his impeccable grooming, carefully coiffed silver hair, expensive suits, custom-made shirts, hand-painted Italian ties and matching handkerchiefs, and a diamond on one little finger—and put him on the cover of *Time®* magazine, between the covers of several biographies and on silkscreen portraits by Andy Warhol. Gotti was known as the "Teflon Don" (Teflon® was the first non-stick surface for cooking ware) because he was arrested for murder and racketeering and acquitted by juries three times before finally being convicted in 1993. His apparent legal invulnerability as a Don and his "braggadocio" under the ubiquitous eyes of investigators had given him an almost folk-hero status.

Gotti was born to a working class family with thirteen children in the South Bronx, New York, on October 26,

1940. He quit school at age 16 and began associating with a gang of car thieves. Gotti gained a reputation on New York streets as a pugnacious kid not afraid to fight other gangs and followed his brother, Peter, into the Fulton-Rockaway Boys (named after a street intersection). By his late teens, he was known to police as a foot soldier for the Gambino family.

Although Gotti worked a variety of legitimate jobs, including as a presser in a coat factory and a truck driver's assistant, he supplemented his income with illegal activities such as breaking into taverns and other establishments.

Gotti was married to Victoria DiGorgio and was the father of five children. In 1980, one child, Frank, was struck and killed by a car while riding a mini-bike. He was just twelve years old. The car's driver, John Favora, endured four months of death threats before being abducted and never seen again. Gotti was never implicated in the disappearance, as he and his wife were vacationing in Florida at the time.

In 1966, Gotti served one year for unlawful entry and grand larceny. Over the next few decades, he racked up a criminal record of state and federal crimes and was in and out of prison. In 1969, he was sentenced to four years in a federal penitentiary for conspiracy, interstate theft, and kidnapping. In 1975, Gotti plead guilty to attempted manslaughter in the murder case of Irish American gangster James McBratney and was sentenced to a two-year term. In 1984, he was arrested on assault and robbery charges; however, the case was dismissed after the victim developed "amnesia" on the stand. "I forgotti" read the *New York Daily News* headline. Gotti was also able to avoid convictions when he was acquitted of charges of racketeering and conspiracy to commit assault in 1987 and 1990.

When Gotti became Godfather of the Gambino crime family, it marked a 28-year rise through the ranks of New

York gangs and the culmination of a long litany of criminal offenses. Along the way, he had acquired a reputation for ruthlessness and fearsome behavior, dealing with both subordinates and enemies in a ferocious manner. During Gotti's seven-year reign, he established the Gambino family in drug dealing, looted entire industries, and "whacked" anyone who stood in his way. Gambino family interests infiltrated the New York construction trade, private trash collection, the docks, the garment industry, and labor unions, as well as gambling, loan sharking, and other rackets.

As part of a federal investigation into Gotti and the Gambino family activities, the government bugged several of the family's major hangouts, one of which was the Ravenite Social Club—a private venue frequented by Gotti and his associates—and a private apartment above the Club. The Gotti tapes provided the foundation of a criminal case, but it was the testimony of a trusted family member that would put the proverbial nail in the coffin of the Teflon Don.

Salvatore Gravano turned on Gotti and provided the most damning evidence against him. Nicknamed "Sammy the Bull" because of his stocky build and gravelly voice, he was one of the Gambino family's most cold-blooded killers. As the former right-hand man of Gotti and his heir apparent, Gravano became one of the highest-ranking Mafiosi ever to turn state's evidence. Self-obsessed and concerned only with the life sentence hanging over his head, he was also enraged at Gotti for pinning murders on him and talking behind his back.

In exchange for a 20-year sentence, Gravano agreed to testify at Gotti's trial, giving up information about the secret inner workings and rituals of La Cosa Nostra. Under questioning by prosecutor John Gleeson, Gravano claimed that Gotti ordered ten of the killings in which he admitted having a hand. Foremost among them was the 1985 murder of Gambino boss Paul "Big Paul" Castellano and his bodyguard outside a steakhouse in Manhattan. Gravano described in court how he and Gotti watched the murder of Castellano and his driver from a car parked a block away. Gotti's rise to prominence, fame, and power as a Don was secured that night when three triggermen in trench coats gunned down Castellano. The Castellano murder sparked a "blitz" of press coverage, and the FBI figuratively signed on as Gotti's "press agent" in anticipation of the day it would bring him down.

On April 2, 1992, Gotti was convicted of 14 counts on charges including racketeering, tax evasion, and five murders. James Fox, head of the FBI's New York office, proclaimed at a press conference:

> The Teflon is gone. The Don is covered with Velcro and every charge stuck. This was really a crossroads, the most important crossroads. I'm not saying it's going to happen in a year, but the mob as we know it in New York City and this country is on the way out. (Lubasch, 1992, 1)

Gotti was sentenced to life imprisonment without possibility of parole and a fine of $250,000 plus court costs. The day of his sentencing, an enormous crowd of his supporters gathered at Brooklyn's federal courthouse. The crowd ballooned to almost 1,000 people with the arrival of seven charter buses from New Jersey, Queens, and the Bronx. Screaming, "Justice for John," and "Free John Gotti," the mob attacked and injured police and smashed cars.

Gotti's popularity with the general public did not wane with his incarceration, as he received a tremendous number of sympathetic letters from around the world—500 letters in one week, according to Gotti. Gotti was jailed at the maximum security federal penitentiary in Marion, Illinois. During his confinement at Marion, he was kept in solitary

21 hours a day—the most restrictive of the three levels of confinement. He died in prison of throat cancer on June 12, 2002. His death marked the end of the era of famous, high-profile "Godfathers," as other mobsters realized the price that his love of publicity had cost him.

Although it continues to remain a factor, today's Mafia is far removed from the position it enjoyed in earlier times. Significant changes in many of the Mafia's areas of interest, and their ability to control them, include:

- **Legalized gambling.** What was once a major source of funds has been largely minimized by the legalization of multiple forms of gambling and its ubiquitous presence. Gamblers who once had to develop covert relationships with bookmakers, numbers runners and other criminal adjuncts can openly patronize gaming activities ranging from state lotteries to off-track betting to legalized casino gambling.

- **Drugs.** The narcotics trade, once the sole purview of the Mafia, has been largely usurped by Mexican and South American drug cartels. Although some of these work in concert with the older crime families, the Mafia monopoly has clearly been broken.

- **Law enforcement.** Law enforcement personnel, on both the national and international levels, have computerized operations that have made it easier to track criminals and to discover criminal enterprises. Due to technological advances in accounting and banking, the Internal Revenue Service (IRS) and its Criminal Investigation (CI) Unit have become more adept at detecting and handling complex financial investigations. Through the enforcement of the nation's tax laws, convictions of mobsters, racketeers and other organized criminals has increased.

- **Federal oversight.** RICO (Racketeer Influenced Corrupt Organization) (Title IX), a part of the Organized Crime Control Act of 1970, is considered the most dramatic and revolutionary change in the investigation and prosecution of organized crime, bringing federal prosecutors into play armed with something more than tax returns. As a result of RICO, mob bosses who had been previously well-insulated from prosecution could now be convicted of running an organized crime family, even though not directly involved in individual criminal acts. RICO indictments and convictions have targeted all the remaining New York crime families. The federal government filed the largest-ever civil RICO suit against the Luchese and Gambino crime families alleging 486 acts of racketeering by 112 defendants in the private trash carting industry on Long Island. Not one of the Nation's 24 Mafia families has escaped successful RICO prosecutions in recent years.
- **Unions.** As membership in trade unions has dramatically decreased, they have declined as a source of money, muscle, and political influence for the crime families.
- **Assimilation.** Early on, the large number of young men who entered the criminal ranks did so as a means of escaping poverty or because their families were involved in the rackets. Today, most children and descendants of mobsters have opted for successful careers in the mainstream of American society and renounced the ways of their ancestors.

Part III
The Washington Spotlight and
The Media Transformed

Introduction

Although presidents have used radio to deliver policy speeches since the early 1920s, Franklin D. Roosevelt's "Fireside Chats" represented the first presidential use of broadcast media in the form of radio to create a personal relationship with the American people. In a series of 30 broadcasts between 1933 and 1944, Roosevelt stepped away from the usual formality that the public had come to associate with presidential addresses and cultivated a friendly conversational style that projected a sincere and approachable image. The Fireside Chats, in which Roosevelt's distinctive voice and cadence were heard to great advantage, did much to augment his already substantial popularity. Still, informal though they were, the broadcast content was sufficiently serious that the public received them as clearly "presidential" messages. Although Harry Truman, Roosevelt's immediate successor, and Dwight D. Eisenhower became adept at the use of radio and later television to address the public, neither projected the personal warmth and affability associated with Roosevelt.

The individual who would prove to be a master in the use and manipulation of mass media and, in the process, forever change the relationship of the presidency to the public was the son of a wealthy family, whose father was experienced in the motion picture business and at an early age began to craft the persona that would make John F. Kennedy a political and a media star.

Chapter 7
The Kennedy Effect

The Kennedy Effect—The Time and the Place

Though in retrospect many of the "baby boomer" generation regard the post-war period through the 1950s as a golden age of prosperity and security, it was not without multiple problems. Immediately following the World War II, the country faced the dual challenges of finding employment for the returning GIs and solving a severe housing crisis. On the international front, Russian expansionism, achieved in large part through agreements made among the Big 3 (the U.S., England, and Russia), was rampant; and the Soviets, through their espionage network, shortly had the most fearsome of all weapons—the atomic bomb. By 1948, the seeds of what would become the Cold War had been sown and were already bearing fruit, especially in the form of incidents such as the Berlin blockade. On the Asian front, China had already established itself as a Communist dictatorship, and the Korean War would entail three years of bloody fighting.

The election of Dwight D. Eisenhower in 1952 brought to the presidency an extremely able administrator and an individual of great personal courage. As General of the

Armies, he had melded the Allies together into a cohesive fighting force with a defined plan for victory and carried it out even in the face of criticism by other Generals and political difficulties at home. Among the challenges that he faced early in his administration was the development of government policy in response to the nascent Civil Rights Movement. The use of federal troops in defiance of the south's "Jim Crow" laws (enforced segregation enacted after Reconstruction) sparked an acrimonious debate over "separate but equal" facilities for black Americans and states rights vs. federal power. Nor was the decade of the '50s free from economic crises and repeated Russian saber rattling. The Hungarian Revolt of 1956 vividly demonstrated the brutality of Moscow's communist regime and heightened tensions with the Free World. The successful launch of "Sputnik"—the first earth satellite— by Russia in 1957 would set off what came to be known as the Space Race.

Despite his administration's accomplishments, Eisenhower's calm and cerebral management style, as well as his advancing age, would be seized upon and criticized by John F. Kennedy when he faced Eisenhower's two-term vice president, Richard Nixon, in the presidential election of 1960.

The Kennedy Effect

The second son of one of New England's wealthiest families, John F. Kennedy's political destiny became fixed on August 12, 1944, when his older brother, Joseph P. Kennedy, Jr., was killed on an experimental bombing run for which he had volunteered in World War II. The family patriarch had made multiple fortunes in a variety of endeavors—including banking, motion pictures, the importing of Scotch whisky, and real estate. A life-long Democrat and the son-in-law of Boston mayor "Honey

Fitz" Fitzgerald, he dedicated his considerable energies and wealth to politics and was named Ambassador to the Court of St. James by Franklin D. Roosevelt. Determined that one of his sons would become president of the United States, he worked tirelessly at amassing political connections to facilitate his aim.

While serving as a PT boat commander during the Second World War, John F. Kennedy sustained serious injuries that resulted in a protracted convalescence and severe back pain for the remainder of his life. Following the war, he initially resisted his father's efforts to move him toward a political career but ultimately ran for Congress and served six years in the U.S. House of Representatives representing Massachusetts' 11th Congressional District. Subsequently, he ran for the Senate and was under consideration as a vice presidential candidate in 1956. While in the Senate, he attained notoriety with the publication of "Profiles in Courage," a book detailing acts of personal sacrifice by past Senate members. The book received a Pulitzer Price in 1957, though rumors abounded that it was largely the work of Kennedy's speechwriter, Ted Sorensen. (Sorensen would later confirm that this was the case.)

In 1953, Kennedy married socialite Jacqueline Lee Bouvier, and the two became extremely popular among Washington's social set. Among their friends were a number of media people, and they were especially close to *Newsweek*'s then-Washington Bureau Chief, Ben Bradlee, and his wife, Tony. (Ben Bradlee would later go on to become Editor of the *Washington Post*.)

Early in 1960, Kennedy declared his candidacy for the presidency of the United States, selecting his younger brother, Bobby, as his campaign manager. Despite opposition from more senior and better-known Democratic candidates, including Hubert Humphrey and Lyndon Johnson, Kennedy attained the nomination and, over objections from his staff, chose Johnson as his running mate, primarily to strengthen the ticket in the Southern states where Kennedy's Roman Catholic religion was thought to be a significant disadvantage.

The Kennedy campaign capitalized on the candidate's youth (Kennedy was 43 years old) and energy as contrasted with the older Eisenhower, with themes such as "Let's get the country moving again." Further, Cold War tensions were emphasized as Kennedy accused the present administration of responsibility for a "missile gap" with the U.S.S.R. As Eisenhower's vice president, Nixon was in the position of having to defend the administration's record while explaining his future agenda.

The event that was to revolutionize American politics occurred in Chicago on September 26, 1960, with the first televised presidential debate. American households with televisions had increased from 3.8 million (9%) in 1950 to 45.7 million (87%) in 1960. The series of three debates that marked the presidential campaign in that year underscored the importance of the new media (television) and, in the opinion of some commentators, decided what was to be a very close election.

Visually, Kennedy and Nixon were a study in contrasts. Kennedy—tanned, handsome and well-groomed—exuded confidence. Delivering his answers in a crisp, articulate "Harvard" accent, he managed to project a relaxed and comfortable image, frequently smiling, even as Nixon answered his points. Nixon, on the other hand, appeared stiff and serious. Under the studio lights, his pale complexion did not show well and, as with many dark-haired men, although clean-shaven, he looked to have a "5 o'clock shadow."

According to later studies, those who heard the debate on radio felt that it was a draw, with both candidates performing equally well. Among those who saw it on TV, however, Kennedy emerged as the clear winner. This was not lost on Kennedy's campaign, which continued to press its advantage in media events ranging from profiles and interviews to photo ops of the Senator clad in a bathing suit that revealed his youthful physique surrounded by female supporters on a beach.

Despite the media attention, the election was extremely close, with the final results not known until the following morning. The Kennedy presidency was, in many respects, a media event. The photogenic First Family received unprecedented coverage from every quarter. The president and first lady projected an urbane sophistication in tune with the changing times of the 1960s. In addition to the obligatory entertainment of world leaders, they sponsored major cultural events and were frequently seen in the company of Hollywood celebrities. Jackie Kennedy became an icon of style and set the tone in women's fashions.

Understanding the uses of television as a means of promoting his political positions and his ambitions, Kennedy established the tradition of televised press conferences. Following her restoration of the White House, Mrs. Kennedy hosted a televised tour. Even political adversaries had to concede the Kennedys' charm. William F. Buckley, founder of the conservative *National Review* magazine, commented favorably on his personal magnetism and his "confident joy in life and work."

The cordial relations that the administration maintained with members of the media were augmented by another important fact: the Kennedys were extremely good for circulation. Mrs. Kennedy's picture on the cover of a woman's magazine guaranteed heavy sales. Presidential interviews, supplemented with photo opportunities, were prized editorial perks. Permitting photographers to capture "intimate" and family moments (even where they were staged) made for great human-interest stories. Pictures of the president playing with his children in the Oval Office, on a sailboat off the family compound in Hyannisport, Massachusetts, or playing touch football with his brothers projected the image of a youthful devoted family man to whom the public could relate.

Beneath the sparkling surface, however, there was another side to the Kennedys. An inveterate womanizer, Kennedy's days were punctuated with one-night stands and ongoing affairs. Jackie's threat to divorce him was only withdrawn after a hefty financial settlement by Joseph P. Kennedy. Kennedy's numerous extramarital involvements included dalliances with Marilyn Monroe and Judith Campbell, whom he knew to be a mistress of Chicago mobster, Sam Giancana.

As with many individuals in Washington, the media were well aware of Kennedy's sexual proclivities, yet continually covered for him. Historian Robert Dallek in his biography, *An Unfinished Life: John F. Kennedy 1917-1963* (Little Brown and Co., 2003), states that Kennedy was repeatedly warned by friends in the media about his carelessness and believes that reports of his activities would have become public in the second term.

Sexual adventures were not the only area in which many in the media covered for Kennedy. In April of 1961, a paramilitary force of Cuban exiles—which had received training, armaments, and funding through the American Central Intelligence Agency—launched an attack on Cuba at the Bay of Pigs with the intention of deposing the Castro regime. With advance information provided by Soviet intelligence and other sources, the invasion force was quickly defeated. Despite long-term American involvement in preparations for the attack, President Kennedy withheld air support in an effort to buttress the official position that the U.S. was not directly involved. Despite abundant evidence to the contrary, American participation was largely minimized in press reportage.

At a 1961 Summit Meeting with Soviet Premier Nikita

Khrushchev, the inexperienced Kennedy was bullied by an abrasive Khrushchev who believed him to be weak. This impression may well have resulted in the placement of missiles in Cuba and the precipitation of the October 1962 Cuban Missile Crisis. When the Soviets seemingly retreated by withdrawing their supply ships and removing the missiles, the general media presented it as a great victory for the administration. What was not reported was the later capitulation to Russia that resulted in the removal of American missiles from Turkey—a far more important strategic move.

The early American involvement in Vietnam and the administration's reluctance to become actively involved in the Civil Rights movement were likewise under-reported, as the press continued to reinforce a romanticized image of the administration with comparisons to the mythical "Camelot." Whether such coverage could have continued into a second Kennedy term will never be known.

The assassination of President Kennedy on November 22, 1963, the shooting of accused assassin Lee Harvey Oswald, and the funeral ceremonies for Kennedy would monopolize television for days, even weeks. Nor would that be the end of the media's preoccupation with the Kennedys. Despite the lack of significant accomplishments in domestic and foreign policy, polls conducted more than 50 years after his death place Kennedy among the top 5 American presidents. Repeated references in the media to a "Kennedy curse" have been used to justify less aggressive reporting on other aspects of their lives—from significant personal misfortunes to the Chappaquiddick incident (in which a young campaign worker drowned in a car driven off a bridge by Senator Edward Kennedy) to accusations of rape (the William Kennedy Smith trial) and other events. The Kennedy family, its activities, tragedies, and legal and other entanglements would create a cult-like following that continues to the present day.

The Kennedy phenomenon was to mark the political scene and its relationship to the media significantly. "Charisma" now became an essential requisite to a presidential candidate, and looks and presentation—often referred to as "packaging"—achieved a great deal of importance, often at the expense of more significant qualifications. That this was generally accepted was made evident following Richard Nixon's return to politics and election in 1968, when author Joe McGinnis penned a campaign history titled, "The Selling of the President, 1968." The cover illustration was a cigarette package on which the president's image was superimposed.

In retrospect, the Kennedy campaign of 1960, and the ensuing presidency, created the image of a candidate who was a dedicated family man, deeply religious, and capable of holding his own with both blue-collar workers and blue-nosed intellectuals. In creating a persona that was idealized and not altogether consonant with the reality, it established a pattern that, in later years, others would follow: the creation of a narrative that transcends the facts.

Chapter 8
The Watergate Watershed

Watergate—The Time and the Place

The period following the death of John F. Kennedy was to be one of the most tumultuous in American history. Kennedy's successor, Lyndon Johnson, was extremely different in looks, background, temperament, and style from his predecessor. A native of Texas who had grown up in poor circumstances, Johnson spoke with a slight drawl and evidenced none of the sophistication and polish that had made Kennedy such an attractive figure, both to the public and those in the media. Nonetheless, Johnson was a formidable political presence and extremely capable of advancing legislation by alternately cajoling and strong-arming members of Congress. Less than a year after the assassination, he was elected in a landslide over his rival, Arizona senator and archconservative Barry Goldwater.

In carrying forward the policies of the Kennedy administration, Johnson overcame the resistance of the southern wing of his own party by passing the Civil Rights Act of 1964, which outlawed multiple forms of segregation. This was followed the next year by the Voting Rights Act and subsequently with open-housing legislation. Despite these efforts, the pressure continued and intensified to do more to advance the interests of the poor and the African American community. In response to this and to demands made by the liberal wing of his party, Johnson launched the "Great Society" program—a wide-ranging assortment of social welfare legislation. Critics believed that many, if not most, of the programs went too far, both in terms of expenditures and in extending the reach of the Federal Government. While some of the measures such as Medicare and Medicaid were popular and remain so today, others that involved the spending of billions of dollars showed no real effect in reducing poverty and, in numerous instances, created programs that perpetuate dependency.

The centerpiece of the Johnson administration, which would ultimately prove its downfall, was the escalation of involvement in the Vietnam War. In an effort to defeat Communist insurgency from the north, the United States initially backed the corrupt Diem regime by sending armaments and a limited number of military advisors. Following the assassination of Diem, Kennedy rethought the policy to the extent of ordering the removal of 1,000 personnel. Johnson, however, reversed the order and increased American involvement under the pretext of the "Gulf of Tonkin Resolution" (enacted in 1964 in response to an alleged incident in the Gulf) that skirted the need for Senate approval of the use of the military. Though initially supported by the public as a rational response to the Communist threat and the fulfillment of obligations defined by SEATO (Southeast Asia Treaty Organization), the toll in lives and the lack of real progress ultimately turned the public against the War, mainly due to the opposition of young Americans of draft age.

By the late 1960s, the first of the baby boomers were coming of age. This would be a new generation with vastly different ideas, values, and beliefs from those that their parents held. Having postponed marriage because of The

Depression and the Second World War, many of their parents were older. The increasing emphasis on a college education meant that the younger people were better educated and frequently more open to new ideas—both good and bad—than their parents. While many members of the preceding generation had struggled financially and were part of an urban or rural culture, the baby boomers grew up in comparative affluence as products of the new suburbs. One result of such differences was the "generation gap."

As the young people experienced the deaths of friends or relatives in a war that seemingly had no definite objective, and understood the possibility that they too might be called to go, protests broke out around the country. With his own party divided into many factions and facing a challenge from Robert Kennedy, a defeated and confused Johnson announced on March 31st that he would not seek the presidency in 1968. The assassination of Martin Luther King four days later (April 4, 1968) resulted in riots in many major cities. On June 5th, after winning the California Democratic primary, Robert F. Kennedy was assassinated in Los Angeles. The subsequent Democratic Convention held in Chicago was the scene of large demonstrations, and the badly segmented party eventually nominated Johnson's Vice President, Hubert Humphrey.

The disunion within the party, coupled with massive social unrest and continuing conflict in Southeast Asia, paved the way for a political comeback that two years earlier would have been considered unthinkable—when the Republican Convention nominated the former vice president, Richard M. Nixon.

The Watergate Case

Both personally and politically, Richard M. Nixon remains one of the most enigmatic figures in American politics. Following his defeat in the 1960 presidential race and the subsequent 1962 California gubernatorial election (after which he stated to members of the media, "You won't have Nixon to kick around any more because, gentlemen, this is my last press conference"), he appeared to many to be a defeated and embittered man. By 1967, however, he was convinced that the morass of Vietnam, widespread social unrest, and political instability had brought about a demand for new leadership. Addressing those to whom he later referred to as the "silent majority," he promised "peace with honor" in Vietnam and greater stability at home. Nixon succeeded.

The first term of the Nixon presidency brought to fruition numerous historic initiatives. His desire to open trade with China was notably successful and capped by a personal visit in 1972. Working with his exceptionally able Secretary of State, Henry Kissinger, he began long-term negotiations with the North Vietnamese that resulted in the Paris Peace Accords of 1973. At home, economic policies helped curb inflation; his environmental policies resulted in major programs and initiatives, including establishment of the EPA (Environmental Protection Agency); and, to facilitate the extension of civil rights, he endorsed the Equal Rights Amendment and Affirmative Action Initiative. Following the successful Moon landing in 1969, he favored a cutback of funds for NASA but ultimately approved a joint space program with the Soviet Union.

By the 1972 Presidential election, he had amassed an extremely successful record, lived up to most of his campaign promises, and was heavily favored to win reelection. On November 7, 1972, he achieved a landslide victory over Democrat George McGovern.

Ironically, the brilliance that Nixon had shown in selecting key members of his administration, such as Henry Kissinger at State, Melvin Laird and later Elliot Richardson at Defense, and George Romney at Housing & Urban Development, was absent when it came to selecting some of his closest advisors. Despite his substantial lead in the polls, members of the Committee for the Reelection of the President (CRP), under the leadership of G. Gordon Liddy, concocted a plan to break into the headquarters of the Democratic National Committee offices at the Watergate complex in Washington to plant listening devices and steal or photograph relevant documents. The plan, which underwent several variations, was ultimately approved by the CRP, by John Dean (the President's Counsel), and by Attorney General John Mitchell.

The break-in occurred on June 17th and was discovered by a security guard who alerted police. Five burglars were indicted, as well as CRP Security Coordinator James McCord and General Counsel to CRP, G. Gordon Liddy. The five were later convicted. In investigating the crime, FBI agents discovered a link to E. Howard Hunt, a former CIA agent and member of the White House staff. After hearing about the break-in through his Chief of Staff, H.R. Haldeman, Nixon became concerned that further investigation would disclose the funding for the operation and attempted to have the CIA block the FBI investigation. The cover-up had begun.

Both the Presidential Press Secretary, Ron Ziegler, and Nixon emphatically denied any connection to what Ziegler referenced as a "third-rate burglary attempt." New revelations would uncover further financial links among the CRP (headed now by former Attorney General John Mitchell), the burglars, and a clandestine group of campaign operatives known as "the plumbers," whose task it was to "plug leaks" and to instigate dirty tricks against the opposition.

At the time of the burglary, *The Washington Post* assigned the seemingly inconsequential story to two young reporters, Bob Woodward and Carl Bernstein. Working as a team, they followed any and all leads regarding the financing of the burglary and the involvement of White House personnel. At the heart of their ever-widening investigation was a secret source whom they referred to as "Deep Throat" who provided information and, equally important, warned them away from false leads. (In 2005, Deep Throat was revealed to be William Mark Felt, former Deputy Director of the FBI.)

As the investigation gathered momentum, members of the administration took steps to preclude the emergence of more information, including making accusations against the media and persisting in wholesale denials. Following revelations by James McCord that the defendants in the burglary trial committed perjury and were under pressure to remain silent, Judge John Sirica responded by sentencing Hunt and two other burglars to unprecedented provisional sentences of up to 40 years in order to incentivize cooperation. Shortly thereafter, Jeb Stuart Magruder, a White House aide, confessed his involvement, admitted perjury, and implicated Presidential Counsel John Dean and CRP head John Mitchell. Presidential aides Haldeman and Ehrlichman and others promptly resigned at the request of President Nixon, who then fired John Dean and appointed Elliott Richardson as Attorney General with authority to name a "special counsel" to continue the investigation. Archibald Cox accepted the position.

Thanks to heavy media coverage, the case remained front-page news and incorporated many of the elements of a soap opera. On February 7, 1973, the Senate established a select committee to investigate Watergate, and the major networks (CBS, NBC, and ABC) volunteered to rotate live coverage of the hearings. When their investigation showed that conversations in the Oval Office, the Cabinet Room, and elsewhere had been recorded, Cox immediately subpoenaed the tapes. Citing Executive Privilege, Nixon refused to release them. A little more than two months later, on October 20, 1973, with events having reached an impasse, Nixon demanded the resignations of Attorney General Richardson and Deputy Attorney General William Ruckelshaus for refusing to fire Cox, an event known as the "Saturday Night Massacre." Solicitor General Robert Bork ultimately followed Nixon's orders and, amid a flood of public and press criticism, appointed a new independent counsel in the person of Leon Jaworski.

As a result of the continuing investigation, seven former aides of Nixon were indicted for conspiring to obstruct the Watergate investigation. Most significantly, Nixon himself was named as an "unindicted co-conspirator." Shortly thereafter, further indictments were handed down charging additional administration figures for lying to a grand jury and committing perjury.

The question of the tapes continued to haunt the White House. Though extremely proper in public as befit his Quaker upbringing, Nixon's private conversations were riddled with profanity. To spare the President's image, the administration proposed supplying an edited version in the form of transcripts. Despite this, on July 24, 1974, the Supreme Court denied Nixon's claim of Executive Privilege and ordered release of the tapes. As expected, the recordings established the conspiracy and included a particularly damning conversation between Nixon and Presidential Aide Haldeman regarding payment to the Watergate defendants. A tape dating from December 1973 was found to have been erased during 18-1/2 minutes of a presidential conversation. Yet another recording released subsequent to the bulk of the tapes undermined Nixon's protestations of innocence and provided conclusive evidence of his participation in a conspiracy. Concurrent with the investigation, the House of Representatives had authorized the Judiciary Committee to investigate the possibility of impeachment of the president on the grounds of obstruction of justice, abuse of power, and contempt of Congress. By late August, a Resolution favoring impeachment was released.

With his position deteriorating and his congressional support evaporating, Nixon was informed by fellow Republicans that, in the event of a full impeachment trial, he would be convicted and removed from office. As a result, on August 8, 1974, he resigned the presidency and was immediately succeeded by Vice President Gerald Ford. On September 8th, Ford issued a "full and unconditional pardon" of Nixon that granted him immunity from prosecution for any previous crimes. The pardon was highly controversial and, in the opinion of many, a gross miscarriage of justice.

Although the Watergate case would recede in the public consciousness in the months and years that followed, it was to result in a major shift in the relationship of journalists to political and other reporting that persisted, with the exception of the Clinton years, until the Obama administration. Long before the resolution of the case, *Washington Post* reporters Bob Woodward and Carl Bernstein had achieved celebrity status. Their reportage was followed internationally as the case moved from coverage of the break-in to the drama of an impending presidential impeachment. In a retrospective documentary on the Watergate affair, former NBC anchorman and author Tom Brokaw comments, "We were quickly in awe of what they were doing." Another who took special note was the actor Robert Redford. Then at the height of his career, Redford envisioned early on a cinematic dramatization of the proceedings, focusing on the two reporters. The fact that they had gone beyond reporting and, thanks to their "Deep Throat" connection, had become leading participants in the drama made them a natural subject for Hollywood.

Following Nixon's resignation, Woodward and Bernstein collaborated on a best-selling book titled, "All the President's Men." In the move adaptation, Redford starred as Woodward opposite Dustin Hoffman as Bernstein. The film was well received and was nominated for eight Academy awards, winning four including Best Actor in a Supporting Role, which went to Jason Robards as *Washington Post* editor Ben Bradlee.

The celebrity status heaped on Woodard and Bernstein was doubtless a factor in steering many young and aspiring journalists toward being recognized not as "news reporters" but as "investigative reporters." This has continued into the present day, with even many local television stations seeking out "investigative" opportunities, both trivial and significant, ranging from exposing minor health department violations in restaurant kitchens to uncovering political corruption. In some cases, the search for notoriety has led to such abuses as outright falsification of news stories to stalking individuals suspected of wrongdoing.

"Investigative" reporting has also been used destructively and inaccurately. CBS Producer Mary Mapes and Anchorman Dan Rather incorrectly claimed to have uncovered irregularities in George W. Bush's military service records, and the possible damage that was done to his reelection could not be fully corrected. Though Rather retired and Mapes was fired, they were subsequently honored by fellow journalists with awards. Cases of false accusation—such as the corruption charges leveled against Alaska Senator Ted Stephens that resulted in a lost reelection bid even though he was later cleared—caused irreparable damage by journalists in pursuit of celebrity.

The Watergate case intensified an already prevalent politically left-wing bias that would ultimately lead those on the Right to seek representation in new and/or alternative media channels. It would also leave its mark on the English language, as most subsequent cases involving deception or fraud would be referenced with the suffix "gate" (i.e., Travelgate, Climategate, etc.).

Ironically, if Watergate was to provide any lesson to those in political life, it was the realization that a cover-up can result in consequences with greater impact than the crime itself. Despite this, as Democratic campaign advisor and commentator James Carville observed, "Of course, this kind of thing is going to happen again." Not long afterward, in the Clinton administration, it did.

Chapter 9
Bill Clinton—No One is Immune

Like Watergate, the circumstances surrounding the impeachment trial of Bill Clinton had less to do with a specific illegal act than with an attempted cover-up. Its greater significance lies in the fact that the story was broken on the *Drudge Report*, an Internet site created in 1994, and altered the power structure of journalism and its relationship to the justice system.

Bill Clinton—The Time and the Place

According to the Federal Communications Commission (FCC) regulations, broadcasters must apply periodically for renewal of their licenses. A portion of that procedure involves proving that a percentage of broadcast time is dedicated to public service. Historically, both radio and TV broadcasters have cited news broadcasts as a major part of that public service. The relationship between the news and broadcasting was first developed in the early days of radio, when newspapers invested in local broadcast facilities.

Given the high cost of gathering national and world news, it was natural that the three major networks (CBS, NBC and ABC) would provide news features on a subscription basis to local market channels that would, in turn, augment them with localized newsgathering organizations. As the public came to rely on broadcast news, local anchormen and feature reporters became "stars" in their own right, a situation that was vividly demonstrated when CBS newsman Walter Cronkite was repeatedly voted "the most trusted man in America." His avuncular style enhanced his believability and, when he began on air to question the viability of the Vietnam War, Lyndon Johnson is reputed to have said, "If I've lost Cronkite, I've lost middle America."

With the proliferation of UHF television stations in the 1960s, and later cable TV, the possibility of alternatives to established news outlets became apparent. The first major competition was the foundation of the Cable News Network (CNN) in 1980. Located in Atlanta, CNN was founded by Ted Turner who began his career with his family's outdoor advertising business. Now available 24 hours a day, the demands of such a news schedule gave CNN the advantage of coverage of events not normally broadcast by the network services. This would result in several notable "scoops," including the launch and explosion of the Space Shuttle Challenger on January 28, 1986, and the 1987 rescue of 18-month-old Jessica McClure from a well in Midland, Texas. It was the Gulf War in 1991, however, that would make CNN a media force to be reckoned with. Focusing extensive resources and live coverage, CNN offered reporting from inside Iraq as the war began and garnered better ratings than the three networks. More than its coverage of events, CNN demonstrated that there could be broadcast alternatives to the conventional network or, as it came to be known, "mainstream" media. With staffs and executives all headquartered in New York City, it was not surprising that network news reportage would increasingly reflect a liberal bias, though this was more evident in special features and Sunday morning talk shows than in daily news broadcasts.

As the political lines hardened between Republicans and Democrats, the proliferation of broadcast outlets lent themselves to a more individualized approach to news. Balancing the traditionally liberal commentators, conservative pundits led by Rush Limbaugh found a ready audience through daytime and evening talk radio programs. Sensing a viable opportunity, media mogul Rupert Murdoch and former NBC news executive Roger Ailes launched the Fox News Channel in October of 1996. Though Fox takes pains to feature both liberal and conservative commentators and styles itself "fair and balanced," the fact that it offers any conservative reporting has caused its competitors and others to label it as a conservative news outlet.

What all broadcast news outlets formerly had in common was their unassailable position in terms of viewers and listeners. Except through ratings, the public was powerless to challenge the major news providers. That was to change forever with the coming of the Internet. Originally envisioned as a worldwide networking tool, the multiple capabilities of Internet messaging rapidly met with public acceptance. For almost no capital investment, virtually any interested individual could establish a site that might well attract a following that could later translate into a cash generator through advertising revenues or ancillary subscriptions. One such site was the *Drudge Report*. Founder Matt Drudge originally published a subscription newsletter that struggled like many others until he reformatted it, dropped the subscription fee, and posted in on the Internet in 1994. Specializing primarily in Hollywood and political features, Drudge understood the value of being the first to publish a major story that could be read by anyone with a computer for free.

The Clinton Case

In 1998, Drudge learned that the editors of *Newsweek* magazine, then one of three national news weeklies, was holding a story by reporter Michael Isakoff involving President Bill Clinton and his sexual relationship with a White House intern named Monica Lewinsky. Drudge broke the story on January 17, and four days later it was picked up by the mainstream media. Initially, Clinton denied the charges, and his wife, Hillary, alleged them to have been the product of a "vast right-wing conspiracy."

The Clinton administration had been plagued by a series of scandals, some of which went back to Clinton's time as Arkansas Governor. These included the Whitewater scandal—a failed real estate deal involving Mr. and Mrs. Clinton—the disappearance of records from the Rose law firm where Mrs. Clinton formerly worked, the acquisition of FBI dossiers of prominent Republicans, the firing of personnel in the White House travel office and their replacement with Clinton friends or supporters (referred to as "Travelgate"), and the suicide—under mysterious circumstances—of Vince Foster, a law partner and friend of Hillary Clinton who had come to Washington to serve as Deputy White House Counsel.

The legal aspect of the Clinton case traced back to a suit brought by former Arkansas state employee Paula Jones against Bill Clinton alleging that he had sexually harassed her while he was Governor of Arkansas. Jones's lawyers were determined to show a pattern of sexual involvement by Clinton with other government employees and subpoenaed a number of them suspected of having sexual contact with him. One was Monica Lewinsky who not only denied any relationship but also attempted to persuade a friend, Linda Tripp, to file a similarly false affidavit. At a deposition in the Jones case, Clinton similarly denied any sexual contact with Lewinsky. In the course of conversations with Linda Tripp, which Tripp secretly recorded, Monica Lewinsky told her about her involvement with Clinton and that she had in her possession a blue dress stained with his semen. Tripp advised her to preserve the dress and, after consultations with a literary agent, turned the secretly recorded tapes of their conversations over to Kenneth Starr, the independent counsel investigating the Whitewater situation.

Throughout the entire affair, the mainstream media focused on the sexual content. Administration figures and Clinton supporters were quick to demonize Kenneth Starr as a sex-obsessed rogue investigator bent on a witch-hunt and to assert that the entire case had to do with a sexual relationship. In reality, Clinton had perjured himself with regard to Lewinsky and possibly influenced her perjury as well. Given his felonious conduct, and his repeated lies to the court, the Congress and the American people, the House of Representatives subsequently voted Articles of Impeachment. After a trial in the Senate, Clinton was acquitted and remained in office. He was, however, later held in civil contempt of court, fined $90,000 for giving false testimony, and suspended from the Arkansas Bar and practice before the United States Supreme Court for five years.

Much of the mainstream media was quick to accept the Clinton position that the entire scandal was a "family matter" and to avoid any meaningful discussion of the legal questions involved. Others on the Left reacted more forcefully. Billionaire George Soros, a major contributor to liberal causes, funded a website tilted "Moveon.org."—a plea to forget the entire Lewinsky-impeachment affair and "move on." Larry Flynt, the publisher of *Hustler* magazine, offered a financial reward to anyone who would provide compromising information about individuals in opposition to Clinton and who favored his impeachment. His efforts resulted in the resignation of Congressman Robert Livingston of Louisiana who had had an affair. Other Republicans who were similarly compromised found themselves "outed" by media sources.

Matt Drudge was likewise vilified by many in the conventional media who refused to regard Internet reporting as journalism. Although the *Drudge Report* contains links to both liberal and conservative publications, websites, and columnists and has not hesitated to headline reports involving conservatives or Republicans accused of misdeeds, many consider the *Drudge Report* a conservative vehicle. Despite this, the *Drudge Report* has become one of the most trafficked sources of news, with more than three million visits a day.

The Internet's ability to present news developments in real time is one of the most significant factors in the demise of traditional newspapers. The speed of Internet reporting, relying as it frequently does on first impressions, is often subject to errors of fact and context. This is, to some extent, mitigated by the ability of individuals or other sites to quickly respond by calling attention to errors. While the Clinton-Lewinsky case may not have been one of the most dramatic examples from a legal point of view, its primary significance will always be that it opened the door to alternative reportage and established digital media as a force to be reckoned with.

The Internet and its many combinations and permutations—including websites, blogs, YouTube, social media sites such as Facebook, Pinterest, Twitter and any number of other digital variations—have begun to exert their influence over mass media and the justice system in a wide variety of ways. In the course of the Martha Stewart case, a website was developed on her behalf with published information, including press releases and defense briefs culled from other sources, as well as letters from supporters. The use of websites, both pro and con, in celebrity cases is a growing trend, as are postings on YouTube. These can range from serio-comic impersonations of the celebrities involved to postings of autopsy photographs accompanied by music, as in the case of JonBenét Ramsey.

A growing problem in the age of digital media is jury contamination. Incidents in which jurors have sought or received outside information touching on aspects of a case or on the law itself have resulted in juror dismissals in trials across the country. Other problems include jurors making postings on social media sites or sending messages on Twitter to magnify their importance in the cases they are hearing and even attempts to contact expert or other witnesses. The increased technological capabilities of devices including iPads and smartphones compound the problem of influence by making it unlikely that jurors can ever be completely sequestered or that legally inappropriate leaks by either the prosecution or defense can be countered or traced.

The foundations of the American legal system were constructed to ensure the protection of the public through the powers granted to the state, while at the same time safeguarding the rights of the accused through numerous privileges and protections. The speed at which technology is evolving and the necessity for more timely rulings by both lowers courts and the Supreme Court may require adjustments that preserve the system intact, while allowing for a more efficient means of prioritizing and acting on key cases. As important as a free and unfettered media, in all its forms, is to the preservation of a functional justice system, it is equally crucial to guard against the undue influence on the law in those instances where the interests of the two cross.

Part IV
Playing to the Media—
The White-Collar Conundrum

Introduction

Given its broad scope, white-collar crime presents a unique set of problems to the justice system, the media, and the public at large. This derives in large part from the complexity of many of the crimes and the environment in which they are perpetrated. In fact, much of the body of law written to regulate business conduct was created after the fact in response to perceived crimes, inequities, and injustices. In the global marketplace, the rules differ widely from place to place. For instance, in Middle Eastern and Asian countries, it is not uncommon for government officials and businesspeople to solicit bribes to facilitate the completion of a deal. In the western world, that would be illegal. How, then, are American companies able to compete with their Asian counterparts?

Electronic technology has also added to the difficulty of tracking criminal activity. In the past, the embezzler was frequently dealing with paper records, checks, and currency in a localized environment. Today, the clever embezzler can easily create electronic dummy corporations and siphon off money to offshore accounts, making it harder to detect a crime. In the absence of a whistleblower or a crime so obvious as to call attention to itself, many companies prefer to cover up irregularities committed by executives for fear of damaging the company's stock price or market position. Even in cases where suppliers or sister companies become aware of criminal activity, individuals involved will often keep silent for fear of damaging a profitable relationship.

Although the public frequently expresses its displeasure at the seeming "coddling" of white-collar criminals in comparison with the harsher penalties meted out to thieves who have stolen much less, the anger is often mitigated by a lack of understanding of the details and nature of the crime. In some cases, it is redirected against governmental or other authorities whose mission it is to protect the public. In recent years, especially where the crimes have involved the more visible bilking of large groups of ordinary citizens, there has been a tendency to impose harsher sentences. The pyramid scheme of Bernie Madoff, which resulted in many older individuals losing their life savings, resulted in a life sentence.

In an effort to appeal to the public, the media likewise has tended to dwell on emotion rather than procedure. When communications giant Global Crossing went into bankruptcy, it was easier to focus on CEO Gary Winnick's palatial office, Picasso paintings, multiple jets, and mansion than to explain his tangled web of financial dealings. Likewise, the depredations of Bernie Madoff were made real to the public through a broadcast interview with a once prosperous couple enjoying a comfortable retirement who were suddenly made destitute.

The delicate balance that exists between business and government is yet another complicating factor contributing to possible conflicts of interest. The affiliation between corporate or union executives and politicians can spill over into the public sector with alarming results. The increased percentage of sub-prime loans demanded by the Community Reinvestment Act and the government mismanagement of Fanny Mae and Freddie Mac was the major factor in precipitating a financial crisis that greatly aggravated a national recession, decreased real estate values, and resulted in wholesale foreclosures.

In a capitalistic economy, business is often perceived as a game in which financial success determines the winners. For some players, the temptation to cheat is more than they can resist and, in extreme cases, can become pathological. In the words of stock trader Ivan Boesky following his conviction for fraud, "All the money in the world would not have been enough."

Chapter 10
"America's Most Admired Company"

Enron—The Time and the Place

The economic prosperity following the Second World War marked the return of many small investors to the stock market. Although the orgy of speculation that ended with the Crash of 1929 was still vivid in many minds, America's economic strength, coupled with increased disposable income, provided a strong motive for investment. Further, a new generation of brokerage houses typified by Merrill Lynch, Pierce, Fenner & Smith, specifically addressed the small investor and stressed a conservative philosophy of diversification. Eventually, investors who lacked the time and/or the expertise to administer their own portfolios were attracted to the emerging world of mutual funds, where, for a fee, a professional money manager would administer a portfolio composed of multiple stocks and financial instruments. As the mutual-fund industry grew, the power of the money manager would forever change the model of corporate management.

Traditionally, trustees and investment managers were conservative in approach and guided by the "prudent man rule" that required that funds be invested with "discretion, care, and intelligence." The new generation of managers was more concerned with performance in the form of higher returns over a short period of time. In fact, their personal income was largely based on their success in administering entrusted funds. For publicly held corporations, this was to spark major philosophical and operational changes.

In public companies with many stockholders, management was generally free to plan for the long term. As long as stockholders achieved a satisfactory rate of return through dividends or growth in share value, retained earnings could be reinvested in projects, product development, facilities, and equipment or other means of assuring ongoing competitiveness and growth over time. With the increasing popularity of mutual funds and other types of surrogate financial management, diversification of ownership became less relevant, as investment authority was now concentrated in the relatively few hands of the fund managers. Because these managers placed their primary importance on quarterly performance, businesses seeking to support or improve their value and to attract new investment were forced to adapt to much shorter time frames.

Efforts to achieve (or create the impression of) greater performance frequently translated into new, and sometimes bizarre, methodologies. The 1960s, referred to by business writer and historian John Brooks as "the go-go years," saw an explosion of mergers and acquisitions. No matter that the acquired companies made no sense in terms of the business plan or that the fields of endeavor were entirely dissimilar, the new "conglomerates" explained things away with such buzz words as "contracyclical diversification." Ultimately, many of the acquired companies had to eventually be "spun off" or sold. In some cases, even this was not enough, and the acquiring conglomerates went bankrupt.

The search for greater corporate performance took on other forms as well, including the use of junk bonds (bonds promising a higher return because of a greater risk) and new accounting methods. In the absence of a major financial correction and the development of advanced communication technologies—including the cell phone and the Internet—public involvement and admiration continued to grow. The atmosphere of the 1980s on a changing Wall Street was well captured, if satirized, by novelist Tom Wolfe in "The Bonfire of the Vanities."

Just as the financial and business model was undergoing revolutionary departure, a social change was taking place in terms of the way many people regarded the companies they worked for. The tradition of spending one's career with a single employer was being abandoned by young managers in favor of pursuing rapid advancement through frequent job changes. Although this had been relatively common in some of the less-secure professions such as advertising, it was new to the more staid areas of business including finance and manufacturing.

Like the financial managers, the corporate careerists tended to think in the short term and were willing to sacrifice long-term investment in favor of better quarterly performance, often reasoning that they would personally move on to their next job before any consequences could be felt.

In the new business world of rapid change and the heightened importance of perception, corporate image is highly valued. Every year, millions of dollars are spent on institutional advertising, financial, editorial, and public relations, charitable contributions, and the hiring of noted executives. The most coveted forms of notoriety include "making" it onto a list of select successful companies published by leading business publications. Within that group, arguably the most prestigious designation could be to be named "America's Most Innovative Company" by

Fortune magazine. One company held that designation for six consecutive years from 1996 to 2001. Its name was Enron.

The Enron Case

The company that would precipitate the largest financial scandal of its time and whose name would become synonymous with executive greed and incompetence began in 1932 with the formation of the Northern Natural Gas Company. Located in Omaha, Nebraska, the firm was reorganized in 1979 as InterNorth—a holding company with assets in natural gas production, transmission and products, and peripheral involvements in the plastics and resins industries. In 1985, the company was purchased by Eastern Natural Gas, and InterNorth CEO Kenneth Lay subsequently became president of the new company.

A genial, likeable man with a flair for promotion and marketing, Lay moved the company to Houston, Texas, and changed the name to Enron Corporation. Ever the promoter, Lay quickly began to establish high-powered business and political contacts.

Enron's early years in Houston were marked by financial difficulties, largely the result of losses originating with its oil trading division. In the late 1980s, however, two events occurred that would revolutionize the company—the deregulation of the natural gas industry, and Kenneth Lay's hiring of Jeffrey Skilling as CEO.

Lack of organization in the production and transmission of natural gas had long created a problem for municipalities and industries that needed to know well in advance what they would be paying for energy over the course of a season. What connections and arrangements existed were effectively dismantled by deregulation. Realizing that an entirely new business model was needed,

Jeffrey Skilling saw the chaos as a great opportunity for Enron.

An exceptionally brilliant man, Skilling received his MBA at the Harvard Business School and had served as a consultant with McKinsey & Co. prior to joining Enron. In establishing a "Gas Bank" at Enron, he moved the company from production to market making and established an extremely profitable—and ultimately powerful—subsidiary entity. Skilling's genius and Ken Lay's promotional skills caused Wall Street to take note. Realizing that ongoing success would involve a combination of continued high earnings and favorable media treatment, Skilling and Lay both envisioned new corporate directions. To facilitate the movement forward, in 1990, Andrew Fastow was hired as Chief Financial Officer. Fastow's familiarity with the energy markets and his facility with specialized accounting practices made him an appealing find.

Typically, the downfall of a company can be traced in linear fashion through a consecutive series of events, resulting in the inevitable outcome. In the case of Enron, multiple factors in many areas, both inside and outside the company, were at work concurrently. Even a decade after the fall, some of the strands have not been unknotted and probably never will be. For purposes of clarity, it is possible to identify four of the causative factors for Enron's collapse:

- **Limited liability special purpose entities.** Both Lay and Skilling realized that, for Enron to generate the type of earnings that would continue to attract Wall Street's favor, the primary business unit would not suffice. Instead, the company embarked on widespread diversification, both within and without its primary areas of expertise. In so doing, it became representative of the worst of the top-heavy conglomerates of the 1960s.

By creating subsidiary entities, and attributing high profit returns to them, Enron could not only appear to be a perpetual money coining machine but could at the same time confuse the Wall Street analysts who specialized in a limited number of industries. Enron's forays into products and services included weather derivatives, water storage and supply, pulp and paper packaging, and lumber, steel, wind power services, water utilities, capital management and broadband, creating a confusing and impenetrable smoke screen in terms of defined corporate activity.

In order to ensure that profits appeared to remain high, Andrew Fastow created numerous limited liability special purpose entities to which non-performing assets and other liabilities could be transferred. In the process, Fastow set up entities in the name of his family which charged Enron hefty fees for facilitating transactions and other services.

- **Questionable accounting methods**. Much of what happened at Enron can be traced to the decision to use mark-to-market accounting. In conventional accounting practice, revenues and profits that derive from a contract over time are booked as they are realized. Under mark-to-market accounting, the entire estimated value of the contract—regardless of its length—can be booked at its inception. As a result, Enron was declaring as current profits monies that did not exist and, in many cases, would never be realized. As new entities intended to generate these profits failed or stalled, the liabilities were simply transferred over to one of the limited liability accounts.

- **Dissociative diversification**. The extent and amount of Enron's so-called "diversification" has been previously alluded to. Some of the most significant projects, including a power generating plant in Britain, a water utility in Buenos Aires, and an incredibly complex power venture in India—though touted as vivid examples of Enron's power and participation in the global market—were expensive failures. Likewise, the forays into bandwidth and bandwidth trading quickly descended into fraud.

- **Success through association**. As a master of media manipulation, Ken Lay realized that Enron would be judged by analysts, not just on the basis of its own performance but by its affiliations and connections. The company's long association with the prestigious Arthur Anderson firm for accounting and consulting purposes provided assurance to many that the financials were correct. Likewise, a web of relationships with leading banks—that were always willing to advance more money—was seen as another sign of financial stability.

In reality, the relationships were illusory. In the year 2000, Enron paid Arthur Anderson $52 million. When irregularities were sensed or spotted, supervisory Anderson executives were loathe to risk losing so big and valuable a client. Bank executives likewise were reluctant to admit that their loans were rapidly becoming toxic. It was easier to hope that things would somehow work themselves out.

Meanwhile, the price of Enron stock continued to rise. In addition to being named "America's Most Innovative Company", it was also considered one of the "100 Best Companies to Work for in America" in 2000. The palatial headquarters in Houston was a local landmark, and the famous "Crooked E" trademark designed by Paul Rand was increasingly visible. Ken Lay's circle of friends and acquaintances, which included both George H.W. Bush and George W. Bush, added to the media mystique.

By the spring of 2000, Wall Street's bull market, which had been buoyed by the success of the new dotcoms and telecoms, was over, due to market correction and a slower paced economy. Enron's stock, which had sold for as high as $90 a share, now traded in the area of $65. As caution returned to the marketplace, cracks in Enron's amour were discovered. In September of 2000, an article on mark-to-market accounting appeared in the Texas supplement of the *Wall Street Journal*. It was read by hedge fund manager Jim Chanos, who promptly conducted his own investigation and discovered serious cash flow problems at Enron. On February 19, 2001, an article in *Fortune* magazine entitled "Is Enron over-priced?" called attention to the cash flow situation and the company's climbing debt. Analyst Daniel Scotto in a report entitled, "All Stressed Up... and No Place to Go," advised investors to sell Enron stocks and bonds ASAP. In a more cautionary atmosphere, the once buoyant financial media was now turning on Enron.

As the bad news poured in, Enron executives continued to deny the truth while privately selling their stock. Much has been made of the fact that Ken Lay, at an employees' meeting, urged employees to continue to buy Enron stock even as he was selling his own. There may be some understanding of Lay's action as, at the time, he was deeply in debt due to a string of personal bad investments and was forced to liquidate his holdings. By late 2001, the inevitable could be delayed no longer, and Enron filed for bankruptcy.

The aftermath of the Enron filing would profoundly shake the financial world and impact the lives of tens of thousands of individuals. Images in the media of Enron employees leaving the corporate headquarters with their belongings after having lost not only their jobs but their life savings prompted calls for reform and retribution. When a number of senior executives filed for personal bankruptcy, and it was revealed that the law would permit them to keep their luxurious homes, public indignation rose even higher. An appearance by Kenneth Lay's wife, Linda, on the *Today Show* during which she stated, "We are broke, we're selling everything we own," did little to generate sympathy.

Ultimately, Lay, Skilling, Fastow, and several other executives were indicted. Lay faced a sentence of 45 years plus monetary fines but died (July 5, 2006) during the appeals process and, as a result, all charges were dropped. His estate remained vulnerable to civil suits. Jeffrey Skilling was originally sentenced to 24 years and 4 months and fined $45 million. Certain aspects of the conviction were overturned, resulting in a lesser sentence. Both Andrew Fastow and his wife, Lea, were indicted. Lea, who pleaded guilty to a misdemeanor, was sentenced to a year in prison. For his cooperation with the authorities, Andrew Fastow entered into a plea agreement and was sentenced to 6 years plus 2 years probation. Further indictments were handed down against bankers at Merrill Lynch. Three British bankers who had engaged in fraudulent transactions with Fastow received sentences of 37 months.

The Enron scandal resulted in the demise of the Arthur Anderson firm as a major consulting/accounting entity. With a number of its people charged with destroying key documents related to Enron and its reputation for integrity undermined, the firm, which had once boasted 28,000 employees in the U.S. and 85,000 worldwide, quickly spiraled downward into a morass of law suits. In an effort to curtail the kind of accounting practices that brought about the Enron bankruptcy, Congress passed the Sarbanes-Oxley Act of 2002. The Act is not without its own problems. Like many "after the fact" government reactions, it places an undue burden on smaller businesses and institutions.

The Enron case is illustrative of the triad relationship that exists between the general media, corporations, and the financial media. Many individuals, as well as money and fund managers, make investment decisions based in part on reports, coverage, and recommendations that they have heard in the media. Television and radio programs in which participants discuss business and political questions and offer advice on stock or fund purchases attract millions of viewers each week. At the same time, reporters and analysts in the financial media community have, as in the Enron case, been among the first to discover hidden problems.

To present themselves in the best light possible, companies spend millions of dollars each year on institutional advertising. Generally soft in tone, these advertisements or commercials typically describe some facet of the advertiser's business in terms of how it benefits the public. Shortly before its problems came to light, Enron Corporation sponsored a series of television commercials. Surreal in nature, some were based around the word, "Why?" and others featured a man clad in a metal suit. Despite the high cost involved in their production and the large amount of money spent to air them, many viewers were left perplexed as to who the advertiser was and exactly what business it happened to be in. By the time the ads ran, Enron's management may well have been just as mystified.

Chapter 11
"It's a Good Thing"

Was the conviction of Martha Stewart for insider trading justified or did it represent an example of "selective prosecution?" One could argue that the amount of money involved was relatively insignificant to the billionaire entrepreneur. On the other hand, the same obsession with detail that alienated many of her partners and co-workers could point to an individual whose greed motivated her to take unnecessary chances. Perhaps most troubling is the larger question that the case raises: Is the government justified in targeting certain high-profile individuals for the purpose of setting an example?

Martha Stewart—The Time and the Place

In the 1960s and '70s, a number of factors coincided which would radically change both the social fabric of the American family and American business. The increasing number of college-educated women—part of the "Women's Movement"—the inflation rates of the 1970s, and technology were factors in that change. By the 1960s, a growing number of young women were attending college.

It was understood that corporations and institutions were becoming more selective in requiring college degrees, and, thanks to increased civil rights legislation and social pressure, there were greater opportunities available to women in the job market.

The Women's Movement, which began as a civil rights effort promoting gender equality, also proved a force in encouraging young women to consider non-traditional professions. The traditional pattern of work, marriage and, on the birth of a child, becoming a full-time homemaker was no longer considered an optimal choice by many women. Thanks to advances in birth control, it was now possible for couples to postpone parenthood or to choose a life without children (the acronym "DINK"—double income, no kids—reflected an advantage that many saw in this lifestyle).

The runaway inflation rates of the 1970s, caused in part by the fuel shortages and price increases generated by OPEC (Organization of Petroleum Exporting Companies— a Middle Eastern oil cartel), brought the cost of goods and borrowing to undreamed-of levels. As a result, many women, including mothers with children, were compelled to enter or reenter the workforce.

In technology, many of the jobs traditionally held by women (telephone operator, typist, flight attendant) were either eliminated or, on the basis of equality, opened to men. Thanks to the personal computer, and later the laptop, most men now type their own reports and correspondence. High school courses, such as Home Economics, that were once geared primarily to future female homemakers are now integrated into other classes or eliminated entirely.

By the 1980s, the various media outlets were heralding the arrival of the "new woman." Business magazines routinely featured female executives who had climbed to the top at some of the largest companies. In order to show compliance with non-discrimination laws, companies now avidly recruited women for executive jobs or promoted existing female employees. Professional associations for women and networking organizations flourished.

For the first generations of female achievers, the success came at a price. Although the role of the homemaker was initially derided, it soon became clear that many of the traditionally feminine skills, including cooking, childrearing, and decorating, were expected even of professional women. When spectacular achievers or magazine writers talked about "having it all" (a high-powered career, a successful marriage, children, etc.), they were setting a standard which many women could not hope to achieve on their own. For an increasingly large number of them, a solution to the problem of keeping up with social and domestic demands was Martha Stewart.

The Martha Stewart Case

If the secret to success in business is to "find a need and fill it," Marta Stewart correctly identified an opportunity and, in the process, became a billionaire. Personally attractive and boasting a record of achievement with which career women could identify, Martha Stewart, through multiple media and product outlets, offered confidence and safety. Her cooking features and cookbooks detailed meals that were attuned to busy individuals. She advised on questions ranging from holiday gift-giving to décor, design and lifestyle.

Never outlandish or "over the top," Martha Stewart's resources—whether in the form of instructions, suggestions, or products that she licensed and endorsed—aided an increasingly large female audience in creating a positive impression and an enjoyable experience. To her fans and followers, she epitomized the American success story and the ascendancy of the "new woman."

Martha Stewart was listed by *Forbes* Magazine in 2000 as among the 400 richest persons in America. Stewart was referred to as the "domestic diva" by the media because of her creative and elegant ideas for home and holiday decorating, cooking, baking, party hostessing, and gardening. Martha Stewart Living Omnimedia, Inc., produced a cable TV show and magazine, *Martha Stewart Living,* and designed a line of home and garden products, *Martha Stewart Everyday*, sold at Kmart stores. She has a mail order catalog called *Martha By Mail,* and she is also the author of numerous books, including *Martha Stewart Gardening Month by Month* and *Martha Stewart - New Old House.*

Far from a privileged background, Stewart was born Martha Kostyra in 1941 to a middle class Polish American family in New Jersey. She was the second of six children, and growing up, Martha reportedly learned to cook and sew from her mother and was taught gardening by her father. Stewart was a serious child who excelled at school and became a member of her high school's National Honor Society. She attended Barnard College for women in New York after earning a partial scholarship. Her first year in college she met Andrew Stewart, a handsome, wealthy student from Yale on a blind date.

In 1961, she was selected by *Glamour* magazine as one of America's Best Dressed College Girls of the year. That same year, at age 19, she married Stewart. Unlike the formal and lavish Martha wedding style, the ceremony was small and simple, with only family attending. Stewart then took a brief hiatus from college to model while her husband completed his law degree at Yale University. Her modeling career was derailed when, in the words of one writer, the "WASPy all-American look of women like Martha Stewart began to be eclipsed by the increasingly exaggerated extremes of models like Twiggy and Jean Shrimpton." Stewart returned to Barnard and eventually graduated with a degree in History and Architectural History. She gave birth to her only child, Alexis, in 1965.

In 1968, Stewart began working as a stockbroker and lasted in that career until 1973, at which point she had the "functional equivalent of a nervous breakdown." Her next venture was to start a catering business out of her basement. She began by tentatively placing an ad in a local newspaper offering her services. Her reputation spread by word of mouth. Over her catering career, Stewart had more than fifty different partners, a number that one "unauthorized" biographer attributes to her demanding, judgmental, and intimidating ways. The catering business led to photo shoots, TV shows such as *Cuisine* to cook books and ultimately to a billion dollar empire.

On October 19, 1999, Martha Stewart Living Omnimedia went public on the New York Stock Exchange. Interest in the deal reached such a level of intensity that the stock actually began trading not at the expected $18.00 but at $37.25, and Martha's net worth soared instantly from $614.7 million to $1.27 billion.

In 2004, following a highly publicized five-week jury trial, Stewart was convicted along with Peter Bacanovic, her stockbroker at Merrill Lynch, of conspiracy, obstructing justice and making false statements to federal investigators. The case involved insider trading through unloading stock shares in a pharmaceutical company, ImClone Systems, Inc., before the price plummeted in 2001. Stewart sold the stock one day before the FDA refused to review ImClone's application for a new cancer drug, a federal action that sent the stock plunging.

Allegations were that Stewart had prior knowledge of the stock's tumble from her relationship with ImClone's Chief Executive Officer (CEO) Sam Waksal. She asserted that she had no knowledge of the FDA action or that the Waksal family was selling their shares and claimed that she had an agreement with her broker to sell the shares when they fell below $60.00. By selling her shares when she did, according to the complaint filed by the US Securities and Exchange Commission (SEC), Stewart avoided losses of $45,673.

Considering this amount in relation to the overall wealth of Stewart, her pursuit by legal authorities and the media seems out-of-proportion. It also seems disproportionate to the billions of dollars that Enron fleeced from the public. Some have alleged that the targeted prosecution of Martha Stewart and the negative media narrative was due to her celebrity status and her status as a woman. Stewart is an "easily identifiable and visible social, cultural and media source in the United States," according to one writer, and that the public image that Stewart has cultivated is one of perfection and elegance. During her trial, the media scrutinized her from her clothes to her handbags. And, Stewart would not disappoint the public; she would stop early in the morning before court to have her hair and make-up done at the high-end Eva Scrivo's salon.

She is also known to be fairly aggressive, and this may have resulted in some people feeling she got what she deserved. For such a well-known public figure, media scrutiny and relentless pursuit of a story is almost guaranteed. The federal authorities might well have taken advantage of her celebrity position knowing that her case would attract the press and hoping that she would serve as a deterrent to others considering trading on insider information. The fact that Stewart is a woman, and a powerful *business*woman, may have also made her case newsworthy and her a target for envy and resentment. In the words of one who chronicled her rise:

> The one-time Connecticut housewife was busy putting together a largely "old media" business of such stupefying growth prospects and cash flow profitability that executives of the largely male

dominated world of "big media" fell over themselves in an attempt to copy her formula for success. They all failed, even as Martha took many of them to the cleaners in business deals over and over and over again, until she was nearly dragging them by their noses through the streets of midtown Manhattan. (Byron, 2002, 10).

Another stated: "She meets many of the gender expectations placed on white females, with one exception, her aggressiveness in the business world."

In reality, Stewart presents a rather polarizing figure to the public: a powerful, successful former company CEO and a domestic diva touting conventional female roles and activities, such as cooking and home decorating.

During the processing of her case, websites illustrated this polarization with a website, www.savemartha.com, developed by sympathizers of Martha Stewart, and www.surrendermartha.com, developed by her opposition. Stewart's conviction and subsequent incarceration may have served to "put her in her place."

That Stewart was singled out for special enforcement is also confirmed by the lack of legal action against other CEOs who cashed out their stocks before a downfall. Kenneth Lay was reported to have cashed out in excess of $70 million of Enron corporate stock before its market price fell. The SEC and the Department of Justice may have felt pressure to make an example of Stewart and show the general public that celebrities and other public figures cannot evade the law with impunity. She also may have been perceived as an easy target.

Furthermore, the media flurry did not stop with Stewart's conviction. Details of her incarceration were also fodder for the press. Stewart was sentenced to five months in prison and she petitioned to begin serving her sentence before her appeal. She was placed in a federal prison camp located in Alderson, West Virginia. The press quickly exploited its nickname as "camp cupcake" and described its college campus-style layout. Author Dawn Cecil analyzed the content of a variety of newspaper articles about Stewart's incarceration and found that the articles depicted a prison routine for Stewart that was easy and in some ways relaxing. They stated that some of the benefits of incarceration for Stewart were weight loss and a potential gain from a sympathetic and softer public image. She asserts that such benefits directly contradict the lasting negative effects of incarceration for most female inmates. In focusing on Stewart's experience as being normal, the newspapers conveyed the idea that prisons for women are "too easy" and do not fit the criteria of punishment.

Well in advance of the ImClone affair and especially her conviction, Martha Stewart had become a media target. July, 1997, saw the publication of *Martha Stewart: Just Desserts: The Unauthorized Biography* by tabloid journalist Jerry Oppenheimer. Some idea of the contents can be found in the first line of the Amazon.com review: "You'll want to wear old clothes: Jerry Oppenheimer's biography of Style Doyenne Martha Stewart is a frenzy of mudslinging." Oppenheimer's book was followed in 2002 by *Martha Inc.: The Incredible Story of Martha Stewart Living Omnimedia* by Christopher M. Byron. Although the second volume places more emphasis on her business dealings, it nevertheless delves into her private life and multiple conflicts as well. In 2003, based on the book, a movie titled "Martha, Inc.: The Story of Martha Stewart" starring Cybill Shepherd was released. The tagline was, "You can't create an empire without breaking a few eggs."

Certainly, one of Stewart's most vulnerable facets was the fact that behind the warm and cordial image she projected in her publications, TV show, and appearances, there lurked a controlling and abrasive personality. Following her conviction, Martha returned to a somewhat scaled-down empire which continues to publish books, magazines (including *Martha Stewart Living*), a radio feature (Martha Stewart Living Radio), and maintain a website. Even in the wake of the media storm regarding her conviction and private life, for many she continues to remain a source of ideas, advice, and inspiration. As Martha Stewart herself might say, "It's a good thing."

Part V
The Racial Divide

Introduction

No other question has generated as much dissention among Americans as that of race. In attempting to answer why the question of race has not achieved a resolution and perhaps never will, multiple stumbling blocks become apparent. In the first place, there are divergent viewpoints and ideologies on both sides.

Following emancipation and the conclusion of the Civil War, many supposed that the newly freed slaves would eagerly seek economic independence. Agencies, such as the Freedmen's Bureau, were interpreted by former slaves as a resource that would supply them with "40 acres and a mule." One of the earliest and most visionary leaders of the black community, Booker T. Washington (himself born a slave), championed education and the goals of "industry, thrift, intelligence, and property." At his famous Atlanta Exposition speech in 1895, Washington encouraged free black people to "cast down your bucket where you are"—in effect encouraging them to build a life in the American south and develop positive relations with their white neighbors.

Despite Washington's extraordinary stature—he was the first black American invited to dinner at the White

House—other blacks, including and especially W.E.B. Du Bois and the NAACP, criticized his stance in favor of a more militant approach. The white community was likewise divided among those such as philanthropists Andrew Carnegie, George Eastman, and Julius Rosenwald who sought to advance educational and occupational opportunities for black Americans, and many whites, especially in the south and among the poorer working classes, who viewed the freed blacks as a threat to their way of life and, among the latter, their jobs.

Although incremental progress was achieved in areas such as education (with the founding of institutions of higher learning dedicated to black students), repressive legislation in the form of so-called Jim Crow segregation laws in the South deprived African-American citizens of full participation in government and society. Even among many of those who supported greater economic opportunities for black Americans, the idea of racial intermarriage and full social equality was abhorrent, and segregation in schools, housing, and other areas was rampant.

Despite Booker T. Washington's admonition to remain localized in the south, hundreds of thousands participated in what is called "the Great Migration" and moved to northern cities where, they believed, prejudice was less and job opportunities were plentiful. The movement was especially accelerated during both World Wars, when labor contractors recruited southern blacks to work in war-related industries. Those workers were frequently paid bounties to recruit family and friends to join them.

Unfortunately, at the end of both wars, many of the blacks so recruited were then supplanted by returning soldiers and left jobless or in reduced circumstances. Although the northern cities were free from Jim Crow laws and other forms of institutionalized racial bias, blacks nonetheless found themselves isolated from the cultural mainstream and grouped together in older neighborhoods, some of which would become urban black ghettos.

Excluded from much of the American experience, the black community developed a separate culture that would make significant contributions to American life, both good and bad. Neighborhoods such as New York's Harlem contained large middle-class black populations, out of which came musicians—who would forever change the course of popular music—artists, businesspeople, and writers who are today celebrated as part of the "Harlem Renaissance." But as employment opportunities contracted, especially during the Depression and post-World War II period, many were forced into greater poverty. The lack of equal opportunities was visible in inferior public services, including and especially education. The high incidence of crime, spurred by the increased traffic in narcotics, increased desperation within the black community and heightened tensions and strengthened prejudices on the part of whites.

In the 1950s, black resentments at racial injustices that had simmered for years began to find a voice. When Rosa Parks defied the law that segregated bus passengers in Montgomery, Alabama, she became the unwitting catalyst for a new movement. Dr. Martin Luther King, a charismatic minister who possessed the intellectual and moral authority to supply the leadership his community needed, became a national voice for equal rights that was long overdue. Although King was adamant in his resistance to violence—even to the point of leading his followers in marches where they were met by fire hoses, attack dogs, police batons, and other coercive means—and did not hesitate to submit to arrest by local authorities, the fervent atmosphere of angry protests was encouraging a far different element in the Civil Rights Movement. Impatient and angry, many younger blacks sought not only more immediate action in terms of civil rights but revenge on those they viewed as having perpetrated earlier and existing wrongs. Individuals such as Huey P. Newton, Eldridge Cleaver, Angela Davis, and organizations including the Black Panthers and the Student Nonviolent Coordinating Committee (SNCC), openly advocated violence as a means of achieving their ends.

Following the passage of the Civil Rights Act of 1964, and under pressure from numerous advocates in both the black and white communities, the national government created a number of initiatives dedicated to improving opportunities for African Americans. Many of these were part of Lyndon Johnson's so-called "Great Society" program—training programs, revision of and increases to welfare and social services, enforcement of open housing, and affirmative action programs whereby schools and employers were encouraged, and in many cases mandated, to adjust their recruitment and hiring policies to provide for larger black participation. Although these programs were seen by many, especially in the white community, as a temporary means of righting old wrongs until such time as equality of educational and economic opportunities could be achieved, they ultimately attained the status of permanent entitlements defended by politicians seeking to attract black and liberal white voters.

With the death of Martin Luther King in 1966, the Civil Rights Movement lost its singular most influential and effective leader. What followed was a fragmentation, extending from the ultra-left so-called "Black Liberation theology" proponents—who preached a superiority of the black race over the white—to those advocating for more and increased entitlements to those seeking to encourage black participation in American economic and national life along the lines originally preached by Dr. King.

That the racial question has become highly politicized has precluded any near-term resolution. What originally began as a struggle for equal rights under the law has, in the minds of some, evolved into a demand for perpetual reparations for slavery and other acts of past generations. Political and social leaders who have achieved their positions, and in some cases their fortunes, by encouraging a philosophy of victimology have no interest in a possible resolution, even to the point of impugning the motives of black Americans urging participation within the system.

In the hope of many, the election of Barack Obama, who positioned himself as a unifying force, would go far in resolving racial differences and demonstrate vividly the quality of opportunity in the United States. But once elected, Obama and his administration were from the first driven by a far-left ideology replete with multiple social engineering initiatives in matters ranging from the economy to healthcare to energy and international policy. When many of these policies alienated mainstream Americans, the administration and its defenders did not hesitate "to play the race card" (bringing up the issue of race when it's not relevant), with the result that divisions worsened.

Many whites were alienated when racial bias seemingly infected the office of the Attorney General and the Justice Department when Eric Holder refused to take action against two members of the New Black Panther Party who were recorded on video intimidating white voters outside a polling place in Philadelphia. The three major broadcast networks and other influential media have been likewise selective in their reporting of white-on-black vs. black-on-white or black-on-black crime. Nor has their tendency to political correctness helped. The racial epithet, "nigger," frequently used by black singers in popular music, by comedians and others, is now commonly referred to the "N word" or spelled "n----r" for fear of giving offense, even in those instances where its inclusion would be a matter of reportage with no offense intended. Still, openly using the word provokes accusations of racism.

In addition to the obvious problems that accrue from political and cultural separatism within a country, the racial divide continues to spawn further problems. Other groups who might have once aspired to become a part of the America mainstream now also style themselves as victims of American injustice and seek redress in special legal protections and other advantages. Again championed by members of the media and employing such recent attempts at remediation as "hate crimes laws," they depict themselves as victims of a society that is largely corrupt, unjust, and run by heterosexual white males.

In 1858, in one of his most famous speeches, Abraham Lincoln quoted the Bible in stating, "a house divided against itself cannot stand." It remains to be seen whether a continuing racial divide and the ensuing demands of multiple self-styled minorities (groups who identify themselves as such in order to seek legal and/or social preferment) can be resolved into one nation administering justice through a uniform legal code, or whether the strains engendered by heightened partisanship will, in the end, prove too much for a union that once proudly boasted, "E pluribus unum"—out of many, one.

Chapter 12
Jeff Fort and the Road to Supermax

Jeff Fort and the El Rukn Gang—The Time and the Place

Since earliest times, mankind has felt a strong attraction to substances that alter consciousness in pleasurable ways. Before Europeans came to the Americas, native tribes were utilizing a variety of plants and extracts, including tobacco, in religious rituals. Tobacco exported to Europe became America's first cash crop.

Drugs from the East had long been a part of European life, though primarily for medicinal purposes. The British conquest of India resulted in a lively trade in opium, and Britain in turn became a major supplier of opium to China. According to the DEA (Drug Enforcement Authority), the first large importation of hard drugs into the United States occurred in the 1850s among the Chinese immigrants engaged in the construction of the First Transcontinental Railroad. Opium derivatives also found their way into many, if not most, of the late 19th century's patent medicines, with the result that a large number of women and children became addicted. The problem attracted national attention, and in 1906, the Pure Food & Drug Act initiated attempts at control through better labeling standards on medicines.

Thanks to improved efforts aimed at suppressing the drug trade and the media's stigmatization of the addict (or "drug fiend"), drug use remained largely outside the mainstream of society, although paradoxically it continued among certain subgroups including minorities and entertainers. Cocaine was referenced by talents as varied as 1920s jazz club musicians (in songs such as "Cocaine Lil") and by Broadway sophisticate Cole Porter in the song, "I Get a Kick Out of You." By the late 1940s, organized crime was heavily involved in the American drug trade.

The counterculture of the 1960s would forever change the perception of and use of drugs in American culture and society. Intellectual icons including the British author, Aldous Huxley, and Harvard professor Timothy Leary hailed the effect of lysergic acid diethylamide (LSD) as "mind expanding." The drug, a powerful hallucinogen, quickly became popular among younger people. Along with other drugs, it was celebrated in numerous songs, books, movies, and in a specialty magazine called "High Times." As the entertainment media (and the news media in general) devoted more attention to drugs, they began to appear less threatening and more socially acceptable. Urban areas and college campuses saw the opening of "head shops" featuring rolling papers, bongs (drug pipes) and other related paraphernalia. Unfortunately, this new increasing emphasis resulted in an explosion of interest in multiple types of drugs ranging from marijuana to cocaine (in various forms) and heroin. The media attention was so pronounced that even grade-school-age children (when curiosity begins) were led to experiment—usually by sniffing volatile and easily available substances such as gasoline or model airplane glue.

As demand escalated, drugs, which were largely distributed through Mafia related organized crime sources, were challenged by a wide variety of new and alternative products deriving from multiple points of origin. The opium based drugs traditionally imported from the East were now rivaled by cocaine from Central and South America, illegally obtained or counterfeited pharmaceuticals, and compounds including marijuana, LSD, and "meth" (crystal methamphetamine) that could be easily purchased or grown or made at home.

A lasting effect of the drug culture of the 1960s and '70s was the creation of a vastly increased drug market. Despite the physical and legal risks involved in drug use and possession, many of the generation of the '60s and '70s continued to engage in so-called "recreational" drug use. To satisfy the demand, the drug cartels increased output to high levels. Despite the best efforts of the authorities and numerous government programs discouraging drugs, demand remained high and entered the social mainstream. Efforts to legalize marijuana and certain other substances continue into the present.

Although the cartels were accomplished in growing, processing, and smuggling drugs, they required a distribution network to bring them to end-users at the local level. In spite of the risks, the big money, ready demand, and low-overhead street-corner distribution attracted many, including and especially urban gangs. In Chicago, Illinois, gang leader Jeff Fort, head of the El Rukn gang, realized that tremendous profits were to be made by combining improved organization with unbridled brutality.

Similar to La Cosa Nostra crime families, urban street gangs claim their territory in terms of defined areas. However, unlike the Mafia, street gangs are rarely involved in labor racketeering, the infiltration of legitimate businesses, wide-scale political and law enforcement corruption, large-scale loan sharking and transnational money laundering. None of today's gangs, such as the Mexican Posses, Chinese tongs, or Columbian drug dealers, have managed to achieve the Mafia's success at infiltrating legitimate businesses, labor unions, and the government. Moreover, no gang leader has been conferred with the folk hero status of an Al Capone or a John Gotti, Jr.

The El Rukn gang is an example of a street gang that evolved into the "first super gang" with a political and social agenda and enormous revenue from the sale of illegal drugs. It had a leader whose megalomaniacal personality led him from street gang lord to ever more grandiose schemes, including the planning of terrorist acts against the United States for a foreign government.

Jeff Fort and the El Rukn Gang Case

Jeff Fort was a Mississippi-born, semi-literate grammar school dropout but was extremely shrewd, obsessed with total influence over his cartel, and driven by uncanny stinginess. He would also be described as a very charismatic individual with a compelling personality who inspired a great deal of loyalty and maintained that loyalty through absolute fear. Under Fort's leadership, the 1960s Chicago street gang, Blackstone Rangers, created an amalgamation of 21 gangs with a ruling body called "Main 21."

The Rangers operated under the guise of being a socially conscious organization, receiving $1.4 million in federal anti-poverty grants to create programs for under-privileged children and former gang members. Initially, Fort seemed sincerely interested in helping the East Woodlawn section of Chicago, an impoverished black ghetto. He persuaded government authorities that the only way to achieve peace and urban renewal in the city was with the help of his organization. The ulterior motives of Fort were exposed when he was convicted in 1972 of defrauding the government and using grant money to buy drugs and weapons. While in prison, he converted to Islam and adopted the name Prince Imam Mulik.

Upon Fort's release from prison in 1976, he changed the name of the gang then called the Almighty Black P Stone Nation to El Rukn after the cornerstone of the Kaaba, a sacred Islamic shrine in Mecca. The Rukns became one of Chicago's largest crime syndicates with some 5,100 members at its height. Although claiming to be a religious group, drug dealing was the gang's major activity. As one prosecutor remarked, "If El Rukn is a religious group, its sacraments are narcotics trafficking, intimidation, terror, and human sacrifice."

The El Rukns purchased a former Southside theater, using both drug money and government funds and converted it to a mosque-like temple called the Grand Major Temple. It served as their headquarters. They purchased dozens of apartment buildings as rental moneymakers and quarters for their members, opened a restaurant, formed a security guard business, and established a political arm. In the 1980s, the organization received $10,000 from the Democratic Party to campaign in black neighborhoods. Members also worked for Chicago Mayor Jane Byrne's successful reelection campaign committee. Fort was even invited to President Richard Nixon's inaugural ball, and the Reverend Jesse Jackson publicly praised the group for taking part in voter registration efforts in his presidential campaign.

As an organization, the El Rukns were insular and tightly organized into a paramilitary hierarchy of generals, officers, ambassadors, and soldiers, staffing a sophisticated cocaine and heroin processing and distribution network. In 1983, Fort was convicted of cocaine trafficking and sentenced to a 13-year prison term but continued to run the El Rukn organization from his cell. Subsequently, when a high ranking El Rukn member agreed to cooperate with federal authorities in their investigation of Fort and the organization, the government began tapping Fort's prison calls and later the headquarters. He would spend as many as 18 hours a day on the telephone receiving updates on sales of heroin and cocaine and directing the distribution of the revenue. But his greatest plan, and the one that would prove his final undoing, was Fort's plot to raise money from the Libyan government.

In 1987, Fort and the El Rukns were indicted for entering into an agreement with Libya to perform acts of terrorism in the United States for $2.5 million. Fort was convicted and sentenced to 80 years in prison. In 1988, he was again convicted and sentenced to 70 more years in prison for the murder of a gang rival. In 2008, he was transferred to the ADX Florence supermax prison in Florence, Colorado, where he is held incommunicado.

Along with the incarceration of its leader, a major contributor to the weakening of the El Rukn gang was a six-year probe that culminated in the federal indictments of 65 El Rukn members on charges of murder, drug violations, and racketeering. The remaining members did not have the savvy or skills to run the lucrative drug-dealing trade, and the gang disappeared. In his rise and his downfall, Jeff Fort exemplified the dangers inherent in the organized criminal enterprise. The gang leader, whether operating from an exclusive social club or an urban ghetto, must constantly balance an array of forces either overtly working to destroy him or capable of turning on him.

Law enforcement authorities at multiple levels are continually gathering information, collecting evidence and seeking witnesses in preparation for the day when they will bring the gang leader down and use him to set an example to others who would follow his path. Likewise, rival gang lords are continually looking to extend the scope of their own operations at the expense of their enemies. From the Capone-Moran gang wars of the 1920s to the vicious battles fought by rival Mexican drug cartels in the present day, it becomes clear that, in organized crime, success breeds an often-fatal opposition. Perhaps the greatest potential threat to the gang leader derives from members of his own organization. Whether seeking to advance themselves in the crime family or through betrayal in exchange for financial gain or for a reduced sentence, the gang leader is never secure from those closest to him.

The Jeff Fort/El Rukn case provides a revealing example of the manner in which relationships between the parties involved, and changes that occur therein, can greatly affect the media narrative. Despite his lack of education and unsavory history, Fort possessed enough charisma to attract the attention of leading politicians and the media even as he scammed government programs. The concept of the "redeemed" former criminal becoming a champion of social justice and finding the means to assist others was and is a potent lure for political figures and media features. It provided an opportunity to underscore the viability of the programs they sponsored and to build credibility within the ethnic community (of which a number of them were a part). Favorable portrayals in and by the media resulted in a story that was both popular with readers and instrumental in Fort's ability to cement relationships with, and have access to, politicians.

The subsequent revelations about and prosecution of Jeff Fort presented a number of media problems. Finding themselves having been duped and on the wrong side, the media quickly needed to re-establish credibility. Further, it was necessary to do so in a way that did not alienate the political figures that had likewise been deceived. The exposition of Fort's involvement with Libya and proposed terrorist acts had to be handled in a manner that negated any charges of racism or inflamed passions against the Nation of Islam (Chicago is the home of the Nation of Islam, as well as a number of churches espousing so-called "Black Liberation Theology").

A number of media outlets chose to reset the narrative by emphasizing the drug trafficking angle and providing minimal coverage on the other aspects. In time, the mention of Jeff Fort and El Rukn virtually disappeared from the mainstream media.

When it comes to the media, the gang leader is dealing with a two-edged sword. Most of those who seek to establish or head criminal enterprises tend to be extremely egotistical—a pronounced characteristic of the sociopathic personality. As such, they frequently court media attention, either as individuals or by associating with politicians or other celebrities avidly followed by the media (as Jeff Fort did). What they frequently fail to realize is the fact that the media, which can be compliant and laudatory one day, can just as quickly turn on them and celebrate their fall in large headlines and special broadcasts or, as in the case of Jeff Fort, with a "deafening silence."

Chapter 13
Rodney King vs. the LAPD

The unlawful use of force by police has been a continuing subject of interest in the media, particularly when the use of force is applied against minority citizens. Although the policing literature reveals that the excessive use of force by police is not common and police use weapons, tactics, or no force at all in the majority of cases, the presentation of a few cases sensationalized and saturated in the media sends the message that it is far more routine. Minorities, especially, are more likely to believe that they are treated differently and that the police use selective law enforcement with people of color. This was painfully illustrated in one of the most highly publicized cases of police brutality, the Rodney King case. The incident involved an African American motorist named Rodney King and four white police officers employed by the city of Los Angeles.

Rodney King—The Time and the Place

Los Angeles has a long history of civic violence involving minorities, including the Zoot Suit Riots of 1943 that involved Latinos and African Americans, and the Watts (a neighborhood of Los Angeles) riots of 1965. The fact that the City and its environs include some of the wealthiest and the poorest enclaves, often in close proximity, exacerbates tensions. Likewise, many of the area's primary industries, including defense, aerospace, tourism, and entertainment, are subject to economic fluctuations. At the time of the Rodney King riots, some of the social issues that faced Los Angeles were widening poverty, racism, alleged police brutality, and homelessness.

Between 1978 and 1982, some 70,000 stable manufacturing jobs were lost in South-Central L.A. with the closure or relocation of the General Motors and Bethlehem Steel plants. Many of these jobs supported the African-American middle class. By the 1990s, the South-Central area was left economically disadvantaged with few stores and a lack of good paying jobs for a predominantly black and growing Hispanic populace. The Census Bureau placed the unemployment rate for South-Central L.A. at 7.1% as opposed to the 5.8% for all of LA County. The unemployment rate among African Americans aged 24-34 was 9.1%. The few jobs available were in industries such as garment making, which did not pay well and were often filled by a growing population of Hispanics who replaced African Americans. Small area stores were owned by Koreans and other Asian immigrants who financed their own businesses and employed mostly family members.

As L.A. was experiencing the economic downturn, there was also an increase in the lack of trust between law enforcement and the minority community. During the period of the Rodney King incident, chief Daryl Gates was police chief of the LAPD, serving from 1978 until he resigned in June 1992. Gates proved to be a polarizing figure with community members and leaders alike and found himself locked in confrontation with the African American community over his forceful policing tactics. He created controversy with his gaffes about Latinos, African Americans, and Jews, most notably with a remark that some African Americans had veins or arteries that do not open as fast as normal people when a carotid chokehold is used. In addition, Gates had a particularly antagonistic relationship with the African American L.A. Mayor Tom Bradley over "reining in his officers."

During his four-decade career, Gates instituted military-style SWAT teams to handle crises, promoted skid row raids to oust the homeless in shelters, and created the CRASH (Community Resources Against Street Hoodlums) program to fight illegal drugs, gangs, and violent street crime. Gates saturated the South L.A. area with police and increased police searches and surveillance of "crack dens." When Chief Gates was unable to control the Bloods and Crips street gangs, he conducted massive sweeps in south L.A. resulting in the arrest of thousands of African American men. After Gates resigned in June 1992, he became a talk show host on KFI-AM (640) for fifteen months. Despite the fact that he cracked down hard on crime and allegedly harassed minorities in his tenure as police chief, he was surprisingly moderate in his opinions as a radio host.

The Rodney King incident in Los Angeles was undoubtedly the most televised case of police use of force, both locally and nationally.

The Rodney King Case

Although the beating of King was certainly not that unusual in police history, it was the videotaping of the entire incident that made it unique at that particular time. On March 3, 1991, an African-American motorist and unemployed construction worker named Rodney King was driving down the 210 Freeway in Los Angeles with two friends, Bryant Allen and Freddie Helms. They had just watched a basketball game on television and decided to go for a drive. Twenty-five year old King noticed a police car following closely and initially tried to get away, fearing he would be arrested for violating his parole (having just been released four months prior for a 1989 convenience store robbery) since he had an open beer bottle in his car.

By King's own admission, he led police officers on a high-speed chase with speeds between 75 and 85 miles per hour for approximately 7.8 miles. Law enforcement gauged his speed as closer to 95 miles per hour. According to police records, King committed more than 15 traffic violations during the chase. King finally got off the freeway and stopped at the Lake View Terrace Apartments. He was immediately surrounded by approximately twenty-one police officers, including members of the California Highway Patrol (CHP) and Los Angeles Police Department (LAPD).

When King was stopped, he apparently paid no attention to the physical presence of the law enforcement officers and police cruisers with lights flashing. He repeatedly ignored police officers' commands to lie prone for handcuffing, a command his two passengers complied with resulting in no further incident. When physical force was used, King managed to break free from four police officers who were trying to cuff him. King was then subjected to two charges from a TASER (Thomas A. Swift Electric Rifle), a weapon with a total of 100,000 volts in 50,000 increments. Nonetheless King was still able to get up from the ground. He then endured a torrent of blows from metal batons. King would later testify to the grand jury that he had obeyed the officers' commands and that the repeated shocks from the Taser prompted him to get up and try to flee.

Awakened by the noises across the street, forty-one year old plumber George Holliday picked up his new SONY video recorder, raced to his balcony, and taped nine minutes of King being beaten by four white LAPD policemen—Officers Briseno, Powell, Koon, and Wind. Unaware of the videotaping, officers tasered King, struck him multiple times with the batons and kicked him repeatedly over a period of several minutes. The beating was illuminated by floodlights from a police helicopter hovering overhead. LAPD officials later announced that the beating continued because he was under the influence of PCP, felt no pain, and refused to comply with their demands. However, Rodney King insisted he was not high on PCP that night. King's statement was later confirmed by tests of King's blood and urine. No evidence of PCP was found in his system, although his blood-alcohol level was twice the legal limit for driving, and traces of marijuana were present.

Holliday contacted the LAPD about the video. When they weren't interested, he reportedly sold the videotape to KTLA, a local Los Angeles news station. The videotape was soon distributed to cable news networks and shown worldwide. Although it was reported that Holliday was paid over $100,000, he maintained that his total compensation was less than $10,000 from all sources. The world saw an edited clip of about twenty-two seconds in all of a stopped African American motorist being mercilessly beaten by four white police officers (with the exception of Officer Briseno who was part Hispanic). The LAPD maintained that the King beating lasted 81 seconds and that officers had dealt 54 baton blows. Tom Owens, a former LAPD officer and a private investigator for Rodney King, analyzed the video clip and counted 91 separate strikes (baton blows, punches, and stomps). Furthermore, he found that the incident took place over a longer period of time— just under three minutes.

During the first week following the incident, forty some articles were generated in various news outlets. For months afterward, the Rodney King beating received saturation coverage in the news media, with thousands of additional news articles and electronic information published.

According to a later commentator, the Rodney King beating contained all of the elements necessary to generate media interest and to create a "narrative of crisis." The videotape was recorded by an amateur cameraman, an ordinary citizen, and showed visual proof of the incident. The primary visual image was the brutality of White police officers toward an African American victim. Many media sources positioned Rodney King as easily relatable to earlier images of white police violence against African Americans, a situation exacerbated by the history of conflict between Police Chief Daryl Gates and minority groups in Los Angeles.

Chief Gates called the Rodney King beating "an aberration" and defiantly defended his department and leadership. He stated that possible PCP intoxication and King's size were factors in the beatings. Despite nearly universal media criticism, Gates was fiercely loyal to his rank and file, adamant that his duties would not be encroached upon. He frequently clashed with elected officials. The media portrayed Chief Gates as unaccountable, racist, and ego driven. Police Commission President Melanie Loma emphasized the fact that Chief Gates couldn't see how wrong and inhumane the beating of King was, and that *he* was, indeed, the real problem. In the media, he was castigated as a leader out of touch with the changing realities of Los Angeles.

The Rodney King incident produced four separate official investigations of the four LAPD police officers: Theodore Briseno, Lawrence Powell, Stacey Koon, and Timothy Wind. A grand jury investigation was conducted a week after the beating, and an FBI probe occurred next on March 12. The investigation led to the trial of the officers. Another commission was formed by Chief Gates to investigate the beating, while at the same time Mayor Tom Bradley established a further investigatory commission. These two commissions were then combined to form the Christopher Commission headed by Attorney Warren Christopher (later United States Secretary of State under President Bill Clinton).

The mandate of the Christopher Commission was to examine the structure and operation of the LAPD, including recruitment, training, its internal disciplinary system, and its citizen complaint system. Further, the Commission also was intent on examining systematic problems in the LAPD, including excessive use of force, racism and bias, the police culture, and formal structures for control of the police department and its chief. The Commission officially began its work on April 1, 1991 and released its findings on July 9.

> The report was highly critical of Chief Gates; found a systematic failure to control officers with repeated complaints of excessive force; discovered significant racism and bias within the department itself and found tactics of intimidation designed to discourage citizen's [sic] trying to make complaints. (Jacobs, 2000, 83).

The Christopher Commission specifically identified sixty-four officers with six or more excessive force complaints, and 16 with eight or more complaints. The failure to control the officers was viewed as a management issue at the heart of the problem, with positive evaluations and promotions given for such forceful behavior. The recommendations were far-reaching including reforms and changes in the areas of police recruitment and training, administration, and organization. Chief Gates, in his book entitled *Chief: My Life In the LAPD*, viewed the Christopher Commission's recommendations as basically an attempt to control the police without any recommendations about controlling crime.

Along with the investigations of police brutality, the Rodney King incident involved three major court trials of the four police officers. A change in venue resulted in the first trial taking place in Simi Valley in Ventura County, a predominantly white conservative community. The jury was comprised of ten white citizens, one Latino and one Asian—six men and six women. The trial produced 29 days of testimony from 55 witnesses. Rodney King was conspicuously absent from the courtroom. In fact, one of the few black faces in the courtroom was Deputy D.A. Terry White. The prosecution felt it was strategically wise to isolate King from defense lawyers who might have laid bare his unsavory past. The jurors, however, had no human reference for King besides the videotape that was shown over and over by the DA. District Attorney White had planned to call King to the stand but decided not to because King's memories were cloudy. Interviews with some of the jurors post verdict revealed that they were unimpressed with the grainy and shaky video and wished that King had presented himself at the trial. They also felt that King's injuries were not as severe as represented, considering the use of heavy metal batons.

The Ventura Superior Court jury was sequestered and deliberated for some seven days. Judge Stanley Weisburg oversaw the televised trial. On Wednesday, April 29, 1992, the trial of the police officers ended in verdicts of not guilty for three of the officers with a hung jury on one count of use of excessive force against Officer Powell. A mistrial was declared on that one charge.

Robert Deitz, journalist and author of several books on the Rodney King affair, contended that the evidence presented at the Simi Valley Trial demonstrated several important points leading the jury to find the officers innocent:

- Rodney King was in control of the situation and could have ended it at anytime. All he had to do was to obey legal commands to assume a prone position and submit. His two passengers that night obeyed orders and were taken into custody without incident and released thirty minutes later.

- Rodney King was not seriously injured. Although it was reported in several media outlets that King suffered flashbacks, dizziness, blurred vision, and numbness on the right side of his face where cosmetic surgery was needed to repair multiple fractures, all medical evidence concluded that his injuries were minor.

- The police officers' actions were in complete accord with department policies, procedures, and training. Even the use of metal batons was acceptable according to the existing rules. The LAPD at that time provided four general officially permissible levels of force. The first was the officer's physical presence; the second consisted of verbal commands; the third was use of physical force; and the fourth was use of deadly force.

Some professionals and community members concurred with this analysis. Rodney King was viewed as blameworthy for not stopping and pulling over and instead leading law enforcement on a high-speed chase. An atmosphere of danger and suspicion was created with adrenalin pumping in all the parties involved. Yet, others still believed that there was no justification for the excessive amount of forced used to subdue King.

The not-guilty verdicts in the Simi Valley trial resulted in widespread protests, riots, fires, looting, and mayhem. Various sections of Los Angeles exploded in violence that resulted in some 54 deaths, with approximately 2,000 people injured and an estimated one billion dollars in property damage. As the five-day rioting broke out, newspaper helicopters hovered over streets and recorded senseless beatings, lootings, and arson. Protesters stormed police headquarters, city hall, and government office buildings, as well as shops and businesses. On the third day of the rioting, Rodney King gave an unexpected news conference in front of his lawyer's home. In an effort to quiet the situation, he stated, "People, I just want to say, can't we all just get along?"

Using race as the dominant discourse for discussing the riots, the media focused attention on a video of a mob of African American youths assaulting white victims Reginald Denny and Fidel Lopez. Truck driver Denny was pulled out of his vehicle when he stopped for a traffic light, beaten, and left unconscious. His skull was smashed with a slab of concrete by an African American youth named Damian Williams. Another truck driver, Lopez, was also dragged from his truck and his head smashed with a car stereo. His body was sprayed with black paint after he lost consciousness. Although the media filmed both events from the news helicopters, they neglected to mention two African American heroes, Bobby Green Jr. and Rev. Bennie Newton. Both Denny and Lopez were saved by these men who stepped into the fray to haul the victims to safety. Both victims survived the incidents due to the efforts of their rescuers, and their assailants were later caught due to the helicopter camera footage. On the fourth day of the riots, marine and army troops entered the city.

In the months following the riots, Los Angeles attempted to rebuild its damaged infrastructure, as well as its tense racial relations. Then-President George H.W. Bush vowed to do his "level best" to heal the wounds and bring people together in the aftermath of the ugliness that was witnessed. In his book, *The Riot Within: My Journey from Rebellion to Redemption*, King acknowledges the involvement of President Bush in offering federal assistance to Governor Pete Wilson and Mayor Tom Bradley, and his insistence that justice be done.

Under pressure from President Bush and Civil Rights leaders, the Department of Justice decided to prosecute Koon, Powell, Briseno, and Wind in a second trial on federal civil rights charges. The federal government's civil rights legal team and a team of FBI agents presented a strong case of civil rights violation. On August 4, 1992, a federal grand jury handed down indictments for all four police officers. All four officers faced up to a decade in prison and $250,000 in fines upon conviction. Two Department of Justice Lawyers, Barry Kowalski and Steven Clymer, headed the federal prosecution team. After deliberating for about one week, the federal jury of eight men and four women, including two African Americans and one Hispanic, convicted Officers Koon and Powell, while acquitting Briseno and Wind. The jurors were sequestered, and all recording devices were banned as well because of the high profile nature of the case and a desire to not instigate a new round of riots.

Unlike the state trial, King made an appearance and testified at this trial. He testified that he did not attack police and that he complied with their orders after he stopped his car. His testimony was in sharp contrast to the picture painted in the first trial of a drug-crazed giant. King seemed mild and earnest and expressed that after the beating he felt like a "crushed can and that his spirits were down, real low." The two officers convicted were sentenced to two years in prison. U.S. District Judge Davies ordered the verdicts sealed until Saturday morning to give the police and sheriff departments time to prepare should any rioting occur.

The final trial related to the Rodney King incident involved a federal civil lawsuit against the City of Los Angeles. King had been besieged with lawyers offering their services since the video of his beating hit the airwaves. Attorney Steve Lerman initially filed the lawsuit against the city. He remarked to the press that representing Rodney King was like being married to a beautiful woman. As soon as the husband leaves, every guy in the room comes over to chat with her and attempts to "steal her away." Rodney King testified that he felt as though he had been raped, and that he felt like a cow that was waiting to be slaughtered. Shortly thereafter, King was "stolen away" by attorney Milton Grimes who convinced him that he would be a better choice for legal representation. Ironically, King ended up re-hiring Lerman after he lost confidence in Grimes. The press had a field day with the legal infighting by mocking King's famous words, "can't we all just get along?" King's lawsuit against the City of L.A. resulted in King being awarded $3.8 million in damages.

Unfortunately, King's subsequent life was, as one commentator defined it, a "tabloid drama" of multiple arrests for driving under the influence and for assaults of his first wife, Crystal, his girlfriend, Carmen, and his daughter, Candice. One domestic assault charge resulted in King's conviction for a misdemeanor hit-and-run. He served short periods in prison and stints in alcohol and drug rehabilitation centers.

In his book, King conceded that alcohol had acted "as the trigger" for most of his run-ins with the law but acknowledged the tremendous difficulty he had resisting its temptation. He was very open about his fight with addiction and later appeared on the television reality show "Celebrity Rehab" and its spin-off "Sober Living." Unfortunately, his sobriety did not last long, and King was once again caught up in the downward spiral of addiction. Gone was the $3.8 million, with most of it eaten up in attorney's fees, some given to family members, and the rest, as King claimed, "wasted." On June 17, 2012, Rodney King was found at his home lying at the bottom of his swimming pool by his fiancée, Cynthia Kelley, who had been a juror in the civil lawsuit that King brought against the City of L.A. King was 47 at the time of his death. Emergency personnel tried to resuscitate him, but he was pronounced dead at 6:11 a.m.

In King's autobiography, he stated that he realized that he would always be the poster child for police brutality. With the media's dramatization of such cases, he was probably correct. People of color view the incidents as the way "police conduct business" in the United States and as further evidence of racial injustice. There is much divisiveness on the issue. The media, through such figures as the Reverend Al Sharpton, frequently cite racism in policing and police policies. Many people of color view police practices and attitudes toward minority citizens as discriminatory and "the norm," while white citizens often view the unlawful use of force by police as aberrant and atypical. Despite police efforts to recruit minorities and to work with neighborhood residents to fight crime, the end result is a minority community that largely fears and mistrusts the police.

In an interview given a few months before his death, King talked about how people would remember him upon his death:

> It's taken years to get used to the situation I'm in in life and the weight it holds. One of the cops in jail said (to me): 'You know what? People are going to know who you are when you're dead and gone. A hundred years from now, people are still going to be talking about you.' It's scary, but at the same time, it's a blessing.

As is typical of so much that touches the racial question, Rodney King's legacy is confused and contradictory, and his plea for blacks and whites to "just get along" is often lost in louder accusations of police brutality.

Afterword
A Narrative of Increasing Complexity

Upon his release from Spandau Prison in 1966, Albert Speer, Hitler's architect and former Minister of Armaments and War Production for the Third Reich, retrieved the plans and drawings that Hitler had commissioned for a reconstructed Berlin. In reviewing the grandiose concepts and especially the colossal structures that had been planned, Speer clearly realized the utter impossibility of his early vision. What made the structures wrong and even obscene was that "they dwarfed the scale of man."

As multiple forms of media have proliferated and affected virtually all aspects of our lives, including and especially the legal and criminal justice system, we might ask ourselves a similar question. Is there such a thing as too much information, too much entertainment, and too many choices for a human being to reasonably handle? Understanding that the "genie is out of the bottle" and that the future will inevitably present us with even more choices, it becomes essential for the informed citizen to examine the legal-media nexus from three vantage points: the technological, the political, and the social.

The Technological Revolution

The basic concept of the legal system that demands an individual be tried by "a jury of peers" presumes that it would include a number of individuals with generally shared experiences—people who would understand and relate to the circumstances of the defendant, the accusation, and the locale. For this reason, jurisdiction derives from the particular place in which the offense was committed.

Not long ago, it was much less common—if even possible—for individuals to isolate themselves from the community and the world. While they were free to choose those types of media to which they were exposed, non-news programs were punctuated on radio and television by newscasts or in special cases preempted by bulletins for significant events. When John F. Kennedy was assassinated, a number of individuals called television stations to object to the interruption of soap operas, so that, like or it not, they were made aware of an event of major significance.

Today, thanks to portable listening devices, communications equipment, and subscription media services, it is entirely possible to remain in isolation from all but the most dramatic events. What many commentators now refer to as "low information voters" are likewise low information jury members. The ignorance of events of national importance has become an entertainment feature on any number of televised late-night or talk shows in which a reporter stops people on the street and shows pictures or asks questions, the answers to which commonly reveal a pitiable lack of awareness. Entertainment has become so preponderant in many lives that even fictional shows find their way into trials (see earlier references to the so-called "CSI effect"), and legislators and even presidents win office on the basis of their public appeal rather than an examination of their record and standings on issues.

Digital/electronic technology, and its ability to be accessed unbeknownst to the user, can present a threat to freedom that can be interpreted both passively and actively. Edward Snowden (an alleged whistleblower who revealed the collection of so-called "metadata" by the NSA and its accessibility by other government agencies) and his revelations were the first indications most individuals knew that their every conversation, transmission, or inquiry were being tapped and kept on record. Even when assured that this was done in order to access potential terrorist threats, many if not most individuals continue to believe that it represents a violation of privacy with potential for greater harm. Just as a photograph or video of a police officer physically restraining an individual can be viewed as either a representation of an officer doing his job or as photographic evidence of police brutality, the context in which the action occurred (which is absent from the photograph) becomes all-important. The same is true for many supposedly private conversations in which an observation, an idle phrase, a wish, or an angry outburst can be extracted out of context and become grounds for serious criminal prosecution.

Reportedly, the late J. Edgar Hoover maintained his position as the head of the Federal Bureau of Investigation by collecting embarrassing data and either sharing it or using it to threaten high office holders. Today's and tomorrow's government officials may have the use of even greater amounts of personal data. Another danger comes in the form of electronic medical records that, if not secured, could be accessed by existing or potential employers, health service providers, or legal authorities to the detriment of the individual.

Even with so-called proper safeguards, the fact that virtually any and all recorded data can be "hacked" by unauthorized persons with sinister motives leaves us as a people open to crime on the one hand and false or misleading accusations on the other. Whether these new technologies will remain our servants or become our masters is a question of singular importance to the concepts of both liberty and justice.

Political Implications

From the earliest days of the Republic, tension has existed between the Federal Government and state and local governments with regard to laws governing everything from property rights to criminal justice. More recently, the increased size and scope of the Federal Government, conflicting political ideologies, and the demands of multiple self-styled minorities have made the conflict more pronounced. One reason for this has to do with the question of what constitutes civil and/or constitutional rights.

Initially, the struggle for African American rights had to do with the need to eliminate and supersede local "Jim Crow" laws. Following the successful passage of the Civil Rights Act of 1964, the concept of civil rights was increasingly broadened through legal actions brought by multiple and diverse minority interests with the intent of using federal power to advance their positions at the state or local level. Many of the groups were astute in their management of the media in raising awareness in support of their causes.

One of the unintended consequences of this broader definition of civil rights is the ability of federal authorities to interfere in local jurisdictions on sometimes-doubtful grounds and with the result of functionally negating the principle of double jeopardy—the inability to bring a person to trial a second time for the same crime. This, coupled with the possibility of civil court actions that are not obliged to take into account an earlier jury verdict, means that a defendant can be subject to at least three separate criminal or civil legal actions (as was true in the Rodney King trials), the cost of which in terms of money and time he or she is forced to bear.

The police officers investigating the 2012 shooting of Trayvon Martin, a 17-year-old African American student, by George Zimmerman, a neighborhood watch coordinator who is of mixed race and Hispanic extraction, was initially judged by police authorities on the scene as an obvious case of self-defense. Zimmerman's injuries were consonant with his position of having shot Martin because he feared for his life. Media reaction to the case was swift, and initial published and broadcast photographs of Martin showed him several years younger as an innocent, smiling child. The media stories brought about angry protests from the African American community that were heightened by comments from national political figures, including Al Sharpton, Jessie Jackson, and even President Barack Obama (who commented, "When I think about this boy, I think about my own kids. . . . If I had a son, he would look like Trayvon").

Despite Zimmerman's nationality, some of the more powerful media outlets, including CNN and *The New York Times,* described him as a "white Hispanic," attempting to fan the fire of racial conflict. A particularly egregious example of media bias was evidenced when the NBC Nightly News, the NBC Today Show, and WTVJ—their own affiliate in Miami—played an edited version of Zimmerman's 911 recording in which his answer to the operator's question, "OK, and this guy, is he black, white, or Hispanic?", was changed from "He's got his hand in his waistband and he's a black male" to "This guy looks like he's up to no good. He looks black." ABC News likewise exhibited a video of Zimmerman after the shooting in which none of the wounds on the back of his head can be seen. ABC later admitted that it had "redigitized" the video.

Zimmerman was subsequently indicted on a charge of second-degree murder and found not guilty. In the aftermath of the case, Attorney General Eric Holder, in a speech to the NAACP, said that he was continuing an investigation of Zimmerman for civil rights violations. President Obama likewise spoke to the White House Press Corps six days after the verdict admitting that he identified with Martin and that "Trayvon Martin could have been me 35 years ago." He further stated that in the United States, black men, himself included before he became a Senator, commonly suffered racial profiling.

In response to the bias evidenced by both certain members of the media and political figures regarding the Martin case, the *Drudge Report* and multiple other Internet sources reported numerous instances of assaults by black youths, both singly and in groups, against whites and Hispanics that went unreported or with only scant mention in the traditional, or "mainstream," media. These included the so-called game called "Polar Bear" in which a young black person would attempt to knock a white individual unconscious with a single unexpected blow. The racial component aside, the ability of the government and the media to attack not only individuals but also groups and businesses on the basis of ideology, political advantage, or concurrence with popular interpretation poses a dangerous threat to both individual and collective liberties.

Although the Second Amendment has continually been upheld by the Supreme Court as one of our basic liberties, segments of the media and the government continue to publicize instances in which the behavior of miscreant or deranged individuals is seen as rooted in their possession of firearms. On the other side of the coin, the tendency of the media and political ideologues to ignore cases of blatantly illegal behavior, such as the delayed approval by the IRS to grant so-called 501(C)(3) status (tax exempt) to conservative groups, has trivialized the misuse of authority intent on depriving a particular group of citizens of their right of free expression.

The authors of the Constitution saw a free press as essential to the preservation of liberty. When the news media becomes the accomplice rather than the watchdog of government, multiple aspects of private and public life— including and especially the justice system—will find themselves in grave danger. This is especially so in those instances in which political ideology prevents the enforcement of standing law in response to societal or other pressures.

When Colorado citizens voted to legalize the sale of marijuana, they did so in open defiance of existing federal law. The Obama administration responded by stating that they would not seek to prosecute individuals who made legal purchases under the local statute. The existence of two contradictory laws poses a potential problem, should another administration seek to prosecute those who violated the federal law. This problem of legal dualism is vividly demonstrated in the context of illegal immigration in which local authorities in border states have to deal with a flood of illegal immigrants and are being thwarted by a national government that refuses to enforce existing law. Difficulties experienced at present might well be magnified in the future when conflicting local and national actions are legally cited as precedents in criminal or other proceedings.

The inclination of ideologues of any cause or persuasion to subvert even seemingly insignificant aspects of justice in support of what they consider a "greater good" invariably leads to the corruption of the entire system. This is especially true when the political sector controls or is heavily supported by the news media. In such circumstances, truth is always "the first casualty."

The Societal Question

Whether the media in general reflect changing social attitudes or promotes them, or both, has long been a subject of debate. Well beyond news accounts presented in numerous broadcasts or programming, entertainment vehicles also exercise great power in changing or forming public opinion regarding national and legal questions. In the 19th century, Harriet Beecher Stowe's book, *Uncle Tom's Cabin*, and the many subsequent dramatizations of the story, did more to galvanize public opinion against the institution of slavery than arguments put forth in the abolitionist press. The uses of emotion to impact the legal and justice system by creating sympathy for or identification with a minority or other group has always been a reality and continues into the present day.

In seeking to personalize their efforts for greater recognition and extended rights, many in the gay community fixed on the murder of 21-year-old Matthew Shepard, a University of Wyoming student, who was tortured, beaten, and left for dead tied to a fence near Laramie, Wyoming. He was rescued some 18 hours later but died in the hospital after six days. Shepard's homosexual orientation was generally known and, following his death, it was revealed that he was HIV positive. Two men were arrested for the murder and, after an interview with one of the men's girlfriends, a police officer testified that Shepard was targeted because of how the man felt about "gays." At the trial, both men received life sentences. The Shepard case received extensive media publicity, and the story of his death is continually retold in a play, as well as in books, films, and songs. The horrific nature of Shepard's death prompted an extension of so-called "hate crimes" legislation. Dating back to a statute passed in California in 1978, and since expanded at both state and national levels, hate crime laws allow for extended penalties when a particular crime can be proven to have been motivated by bias against race, religion, national origin, and, since the Matthew Shepard Act, gender, gender identity, sexual orientation, and disability. Hate crime laws are not without their detractors who believe that they cross the line by penalizing individuals for thoughts and feelings, irrespective of their criminal acts. Where a hate crime is verified by an individual's prior speech, many believe that this constitutes a violation of the First Amendment and that punishment should address the crime itself regardless of the motivating factors, no matter how socially abhorrent they are.

Matthew Shepard remains a martyr figure despite the fact that a recent book (*The Book of Matt: Hidden Truths about the Murder of Matthew Shepard*) by Stephen Jaminez, an admitted gay man, reveals that the murderers were not strangers, as had been stated, but that his killer, Aaron McKinney, had engaged in sex with Shepard, that both men were drug dealers, and that the murder was motivated by a drug deal gone bad. Despite this, it is largely remembered as a hate crime.

As with hate crimes, other societal changes can have the impact of curtailing long-standing rights through regulations and laws if not outright criminalization. The Affordable Care Act demands that Catholic and other institutions opposed to abortion on moral grounds provide for the distribution of birth control means, including abortifacients, in or through their insurance plans for employees. The debate over abortion continues to be one of the most emotional in history with no perceived resolution in sight and multiple contradictory factors. In a highly publicized trial, California resident Scott Peterson was sentenced to death for the murder of his 8-month-pregnant wife, Laci, exacerbated by the death of their unborn son. Ordinarily, murder in California cannot carry the death penalty. Yet, had Laci wished, she could have aborted the fetus without penalty. Further, in civil suits, recovery can be awarded if it can be proven that an unborn child was damaged through negligence or other means.

Unquestionably, evolving social attitudes can exert a profound effect on the justice system, and the debate continues as to whether or to what extent the system should adapt to the changes or whether, in the long run, rights are better safeguarded through the preservation of the initial interpretations of the law—something that can become extremely hard in the face of media pressure. In Great Britain, which has seen a large influx of Muslims, certain judges have opted to consider Sharia Law as opposed to relying strictly on the Codes of the United Kingdom. In the United States, at least one Supreme Court justice, Ruth Bader Ginsberg, has opined that we should take international law into account, even where it conflicts with our own statutes.

In establishing the foundations of the American legal system, the Founders were well aware of the effects of societal pressures on law. Intent on the preservation of religious freedom, they were concerned about the undue influences of state religions and theocracies on both personal and national liberty. Their concern for the rights and liberty of the individual can be seen throughout the Bill of Rights—the first ten amendments to the Constitution. Having themselves experienced the effects of an authoritarian government, they were determined to define law in such a way as to protect the dignity of the individual, even going so far as to forbid the use of "cruel and unusual punishments."

At the same time, the system was designed to protect the rights of the majority and to seek those remedies or prohibitions that resulted in the greatest good to the largest number. The motto "E pluribus unum" (out of many, one), which originally referenced the assimilation of 13 colonies into one nation, would ultimately, in the popular mind, come to serve as an illustration of America's "melting pot" culture, wherein immigrants would willingly shed their minority status in favor of an identification as "Americans." Even from a racial standpoint, the speeches and writings of Dr. Martin Luther King make it abundantly clear that the assimilation of African Americans into the mainstream of American life was his primary goal.

In more recent times, as minority status has conferred special privileges on certain groups, including specific laws for their protection, we have seen radical changes in both society and the legal system, which have been championed, in many cases, by all forms of the media. A number of these have come at the expense of other groups, creating a "political correctness" that threatens many of our oldest and most cherished liberties, chief among them freedom of speech.

Where minority interests have, for whatever reason, become a chief concern of government, the result is generally the inception of any number of separatist movements, either by those seeking a more advanced status or others who reject the minority preferment. The fact that politically correct movements can gain the favor and support of certain members of the media is in no small way responsible for the divisiveness that follows. Clearly, the multiple technological, political, and social changes will, at least philosophically, require a redefinition of the relationship between the general media and the justice system on an ethical and moral basis to ensure that the rights of the individual or the group caught between the two can and will be preserved.

REFERENCES

Allen, L. *Being Martha: The Inside Story of Martha Stewart and Her Amazing Life*. Hoboken, NJ: John Wiley & Sons, Inc., 2006.

Anonymous. King Still Largely an Enigma. *Sentinel*, April 11, 1993, A4.

———. Rodney King Testifies About Night of Beating. *New York Times,* January 22 1993, A16.Baird, J.E. and Bradley, P.H. (1979). Styles of Management and Communication: A Comparative Study of Men and Women. *Communication Monograph, 46*, 101-111.

Baker, P.R. *Stanny: The Gilded Life of Stanford White*. The Free Press (a division of Macmillan Inc., New York, 1989.

Barak, G. *Representing O.J.: the trial of the twentieth century*. In F.Y. Bailey and S. Chermak. *Famous American Crimes and Trials*. Westport, CT: Praeger Publishers (2004). pp. 189-207.

Bernstein, C. and B. Woodward. *All the President's Men*. New York: Simon & Schuster, 1974.

Bosco, Joseph. *A Problem of Evidence*. New York: William Morrow & Co., 1996.

Boynton, G. "Ted Bundy: The serial killer next door." In Bailey, F.Y. and Chermak, S. (Eds.). *Famous Crimes and Trials. Vol. 4-1960-1980.* Westport, CT: Praeger (2004), 251-272.

Brightman, H.J. *Today's White Collar Crime. Legal, Investigative, and Theoretical Perspectives*. New York, NY: Routledge, 2009.

Brooks, J. *The Go-Go Years*. Wiley, 1999.Burton, Richard F. Translation. *The Arabian Nights: Tales from a Thousand and One Nights*. New York: Modern Library Classics, 2001.

———. *The seven fat years;: Chronicles of Wall Street.* New York: Harper and Bros, 1958.

Bugliosi, V. *Outrage: The Five Reasons Why O.J. Simpson Got Away with Murder.* New York: W.W. Norton & Co., Inc., 1996.

Byron, C.M. *Martha, Inc. The Incredible Story of Martha Stewart Living Omnimedia.* New York: John Wiley & Sons, Inc., 2002.

Cecil, D.K. Doing time in "Camp Cupcake": Lessons learned from newspaper accounts of Martha Stewart's Incarceration. Journal of Criminal Justice and Popular Culture (2007), 14(2), 142-160.

Chermak, S. "Body count news: How crime is presented in the news. *News Media Quarterly* (1994), 11(4): 561-582.

———. *Victims in the News. Crime in American News Media.* Boulder, CO: Westview Publishing. Cohen, P. (1998). *The Murder of Helen Jewett.* New York: Alfred A. Knopf, Inc., 1995.

Coffey, K. *Spinning the Law.* New York: Prometheus Books, 2010.

Cooley, Amanda and Bess Carrie and Marsh Rubin-Jackson with Tom Byrnes and Mike Wallace. *Madame Foreman.* Beverly Hills: Dove Books, 1995.

Coon, S.C. with R. Dietz. *Presumed Guilty. The Tragedy of the Rodney King Affair.* Washington, D.C.: Regnery Gateway, 1992.

Cullen, D. *Columbine.* New York: Hatchet Book Group, 2009.

Crier, C. *A Deadly Game.* New York: Regan Books, 2005.

Dallek, R. *An Unfinished Life: John F. Kennedy 1917-1963.* New York: Little Brown and Co., 2003.

Darden, Christopher, and Jess Walter. *In Contempt.* New York: Harper, 1996.

Dash, M. *The First Family*. New York: Random House, 2009.

Davies, G.K. Connecting the Dots. Lessons From the Virginia Tech Shootings. *Change,* January/February (2008), 9-15.

Dershowitz, Alan M. *Reasonable Doubts*. New York: Touchstone, 1996.

Deitz, R. A Few Facts in the Rodney King Case. *The Wall Street Journal,* August 14, 1992, 10.

———. A closer Look at Rodney King. *The Dallas Morning News. Home Final Edition,* February, 1993, 13A.

———. *Willful Injustice: A Post-O.J. Look at the Rodney King, American Justice and Trial by Race.* Washington, D.C.: Regnery Publishing, Inc., 1996.

de Tocqueville, A. *Democracy in America*. Library of America. 2004: Literary Classics of the United States, Inc. New York, New York, 1851.

Deutsch, S.K. and G. Cavender. CSI and forensic realism. *Journal of Criminal Justice and Popular Culture* (2008), *15*(1): 34-53

Dickens, Charles. *The Old Curiosity Shop*. England: Chapman and Hall, 1841.

Dillon, Nancy. O.J. friend says Simpson's idea to use firearms. *New York Daily News,* October 18, 2007.

Dinkes, R., E.F. Cataldi, G. Kent, and K. Baum. (2006). *Indicators of School Crime and Safety.* Washington, D.C. : U.S. Department of Justice and U.S. Department of Education. Dautrich, K. and T. H. Hartley. *How the News Media Fail American Voters. Causes, Consequences and Remedies.* New York: Columbia University Press, 1999.

Dominick, J. On Daryl Gates; L.A. changed, but he…and his department….would not. *Los Angeles Times,* April 17, 2010, A31.

Edelhertz, H. The Nature, Impact and Prosecution of White Collar Crime (ICR 70-71). Washington, DC: U.S. Department of Justice, 1970.

Edgerton, R. B. The California Nightmare. *National Review* (1998), 50(17), 52.

Edmonds, A. *Frame-Up! The Untold Story of Roscoe "Fatty" Arbuckle*. New York: Wm. Morrow & Co., 1991.

Egger, S. "A working definition of serial murder and the reduction of linkage blindness. *Journal of Police Science and Administration* (1984), 12(3):348-357.

————.*The Need to Kill. Inside the World of the Serial Killer*. Saddle River, NJ: Prentice Hall, 2003.

Egger, K. and Egger, S. Victims of serial killers. The less dead. In (Sgarzi, J. and McDevitt, J.(Eds.). *Victimology. A Study of Crime Victims and Their Roles*. Upper Saddle River, NJ: Prentice Hall (2003), 99-32.

Elicker, M.K. Unlawful justice: An American study of police use of force and how views changed based on race and occupation, *Sociological Viewpoints* (2008), 24, 33-49.

Fast, J. *Ceremonial Violence. A Psychological Explanation of School Shootings*. Woodstock, NY: Overlook Press, 2008.

Fisher, J. *The Lindbergh Case*. New Jersey: Rutgers University Press, 1994.

Flood, M. and T. Fowler. Grand Jurors Eye Lay; #70 Million in Stock Sales Focus of Probe. *Houston Chronicle*, October 24, 2002.

Fox, C., D. J. Harding, J. Mehta, and W. Roth. *Rampage. The Social Roots of School Shootings*. New York: Basic Books, 2004.

Franke, D. *The Torture Doctor*. Hawthorn Books, 1975.

Gaber, D. *Crime News and the Public*. New York: Praeger, 1980.

Gamson, W.A, D. Croteau, W. Haven, and T. Sassor.(1992). "Media images and the social construction of reality. *Annual Review of Sociology* (1992), 18, 373-393.

Garner, J. We Interrupt this Broadcast. The Events that Stopped Our Lives. From the Hindenburg Explosion to the Virginia Tech Shooting. Naperville, IL: Sourcebook Media, 2008.

————. *We Interrupt This Broadcast*. Naperville, Ill: Sourcebooks MediaFusion (2008).

Gibson, D. C. *Serial murder and media circuses.* Westport, CT: Praeger Publishers, 2005.

Gilfoyle, T. *City of Eros.* New York: W.W Norton & Company, Inc., 1992.

Goode, E. and N. Ben-Yehuda. "Moral Panics: Culture, Politics and Social Construction." *Annual Review of Sociology* (1994), 20, 149-171.

Gray, M. The LA Riots: 15 years after the Rodney King. *Time* (2007), 1.

Halberstam, D. *The Fifties.* New York: Villard Brooks, 1993.

Heminway, Joan MacLeod. Save Martha Stewart? Observations about Equal Justice in U.S. Insider Trading Regulation. Texas Journal of Women and the Law (2003) 12(2), 247-285.

Hersh, S.M. *The Dark Side of Camelot.* New York: Little, Brown and Co., 1997.

Hill, G. & K. *The People's Law Dictionary.* MJF Books, 2002.

Hodgson, G., B. Page and C. Raw. *Do You Sincerely Want to be Rich?* Viking Press, Inc., 1971.

Hone, P. *The Diary of Philip Hone (1828-1851).* Arno and The New York Times, 1927.

Huffstutter, P.G. and S. Simon. Media's role in BTK case scrutinized. *Los Angeles Times,* March 4, 2005, Part A, p. 2.

Hughes, T. and M. Magers. "The perceived impact of crime scene investigation shows on the administration of justice." *Journal of Criminal Justice and Popular Culture* (2007), 14(3): 259-276.

Humphries, D. "Serious crime and, news coverage and ideology. A content analysis of crime coverage in a metropolitan paper." *Crime and Delinquency* (1981), :191-205.

Hunt, D.M. *O.J. Simpson Facts and Fictions: News Rituals in the Construction of Reality*. Cambridge, U.K.: Cambridge University Press (1999).

Jacobs, R.N. Civil society and crisis. Culture, discourse and the Rodney King beating. *American Journal of Sociology* (1996), 101(5): 1238-1272.

———. *Race, Media and the Crisis of Civil Society. From Watts to Rodney King*. Cambridge: Cambridge University Press, 2000.

James, D. Black History. Cops Gone Wild. *Sentinel,* Los Angeles, February 19, 2009, A7, A13.

Jenkins, H.W. An Autumnal Resolution: Give Martha a Break. *The Wall Street Journal*, September 4, 2002, A23.

Jesiek, B.K. and J. Hunsinger. The April 16 Archive: Collecting and Preserving Memories of the Virginia Tech Tragedy. In Agger, B. and Luke, J.W. (Eds.). There is a Gunman on Campus. Tragedy and Terror at Virginia Tech. Lanham, MD: Rowman and Littlefield Publishers (2008), pp 185-206.

Jimeney, S. *The Book of Matt: Hidden Truths About the Murder of Matthews Shepard*. Hanover, NH: Steerforth Press, 2013.

Jones, T.L. *The O.J. Simpson Murder Trial*. Marilyn Bardsley, Rachael Bell. *Crime Library on truTV* (2008). An excellent and compact chronology of the trial as well as several appendixes covering subsequent events through 2008. In addition to previously quoted sources, the authors cite the following:

Kappler, V.E., M. Blumberg and G. W. Potter. *The Mythology of Crime and Criminal Justice.* Prospect Heights, Il: Waveland Press. Small, M. and Dressler Terrick, K. (2001). *School Violence" An Overview.* Washington, D.C.: Office of Juvenile Justice and Delinquency Prevention (2000), 3-12.

Kasinsky, R.G. "Patrolling the facts: Media, Cops and crime." In Barak, G. (Ed.). *Media, Process and the Social Construction of Crime.* New York: Garland Publishing (1994), 203-234.

Kellner, D. Media Spectacle and the Massacre at Virginia Tech. In Agger, B. and Luke, J.W. (Eds.). There is a Gunman on Campus. Tragedy and Terror at Virginia Tech. Lanham, MD: Rowman and Littlefield Publishers (2008), pp 29-54.

Kennedy, L. *The Airman and the Carpenter.* New York: Penguin Books, 1986.

Killingbeck, D. "The Role of Television News in the Construction of School Violence as a Moral Panic." In Potter, G.W. and V.E. Kappeler (Eds.). *Constructing Crime.* Long Grove, Il: Waveland Press (2006), 213-247.

King, R. and L.J. Spagnola. *The Riot Within: My journey from rebellion to redemption.* New York: HarperCollins Publishers, 2012.

Kobler, J. *Capone: The Life and World of Al Capone.* New York: Da Capo Press, 2003.

Koons, S. and R. Dietz. *Presumed Guilty: The Tragedy of the Rodney King Affair.* Washington, D.C: Regnery Gateway Publishing, 1992.

Lampe, P. *The Mother Teresa Syndrome.* Holland: Nelissen, 2002.

Lange, Tom and Phil. Vannatter with Dan E. Moldea. *Evidence Dismissed.* New York: Simon & Schuster, 1997.

Langford, G. *The Murder of Stanford White.* Bobbs-Merrrill Co. Inc., 1962.

Langman, P. *Why Kids Kill. Inside the Minds of School Shooters.* New York: Palgrave Macmillan, 2009.

Lardner, J. and T. Reppetto. *NYPD: A City and Its Police.* Henry Holt and Co. New York, 2000.

Larkin, R.W. *Comprehending Columbine.* Philadelphia, PA: Temple University Press, 2007.

Larson, E. *The Devil in the White City.* New York: Crown, 2003.

Leduff, C. 12 Years After the Riots, Rodney King Gets Along. *New York Times,* September 19, 2004, 1, 22.

Lessard, S. *The Architect of Desire: Beauty and Danger in the Stanford White Family.* The Dial Press. New York, 1996.

Lester, D. *Serial Killers. The Insatiable Passion.* Charles Press Publishers: Philadelphia, PA, 1995.

Loden, R. *Feminine Leadership or How to Succeed in Business Without Being One of the Boys.* New York: Times Books, 1985.

Los, M. and S.E. Chamard. Selling newspaper or education the public? Sexual violence in the media. *Canadian Journal of Criminology* (1997), 39(3): 293-328.

Lynn, K. Martha Stewart Trial for Insider Trading; Here's a Review of Case. *The Record* (New Jersey) (February 5, 2004).

Martin, B. The beating of Rodney King: The dynamics of backfire. *Critical Criminology* (2005), 13(3):307-326.

Mauro, T. Anatomy of a Trial: How the Scales Tipped to "Not Guilty"/ Juror's Reply to Critics: You Weren't There. *USA Today,* May 6, 1992, 1A.

McClam, E. and A. D'Innocenzio. Guilty on All Counts: Stewart to Appeal. *The Gazette* (Montreal, Quebec), March 6, 2004, B1.

McCluhan, M. *Understanding Media: The Extensions of Man.* McGraw-Hill, 1964.

McCluhan, M. *The Medium is the Message: An Inventory of Effects.* Random House, 1967.

McLean, B. and P. Elkind, P. *The Smartest Guys in the Room.* New York, NY: Portfolio, member of Penguin Group (USA) Inc., 2003.

Medina, J. Rodney King Dies at the age of 47; Police beating victim who asked, "Can we all get along?" *New York Times,* June 17, 2012, 1-4.

Michaud, S.G. and H. Aynesworth. *Ted Bundy. Conversations with a Killer.* New York, NY: A Signet Book, 1989.

Mitchell, J.L. Rodney King, The Man Occupies Center Stage as Jury Ponders Character Issue. *Los Angeles Times,* April 17, 1994, A 10.

Moore, N.Y. and L. Williams. *The Almighty Black P Stone Nation, The Rise, Fall, and Resurgence of an American Gang.* Chicago: Lawrence Hill Books, 2011.

Morrison, Toni and Claudia Brodsky Lacour. *Birth of a Nation'hood.* New York: Random House, 1997.

Muraskin, R. and S. Feuer Domash. *Crime and the Media: Headlines vs. Reality.* Upper Saddle River, NJ: Prentice Hall, 2007.

NAACP. *Beyond the Rodney King Story. An Investigation of Police Misconduct in Minority Communities.* Boston: Northeastern University Press, 1995.

Ogilvy, D. *Ogilvy on Advertising.* New York: Vintage Books, 1985.

Oppenheimer, J. *Martha Stewart: Just Desserts: The Unauthorized Biography.* New York: William Morrow and Company, Inc., 1997.

Owens, T. with R. Browning. *Lying Eyes. Behind the Corruption and Brutality of the LAPD and the Beating of Rodney King.* New York: Thunder's Mouth Press, 1994.

Palermo, G.B. and M.A. Farkas. *The Dilemma of the Sexual Offender.* Springfield, Ill: Charles C. Thomas Publisher, 2001.

―――. *The Dilemma of the Sexual Offender. Second Edition.* Charles C. Thomas Publisher (2013), pp.1-321.

Paul, Raymond. *Who Murdered Mary Rogers?* Prentice Hall, 1971.

Pizzato, M. (1999). "Jeffrey Dahmer and Media Cannibalism. The Lure and Failure of Sacrifice." In Sharrett, C. (Ed.). *My theologies of Violence in Postmodern Media.* Detroit, MI: Wayne State University Press, 85-118.

Poe, E. A. "The Mystery of Marie Roget" (story with footnotes) in *Edgar Allan Poe: Poetry and Tales,* The Library of America, 1984.

Potter, G.W. and V.E. Kappeler. *Constructing Crime: Perspective on Making News and Social Problems.* Long Grove, IL: Waveland Press, 2006.

Puente, M. Police Chief Gates: No Winners in King Case. *USA Today,* April 30, 1992, 3A.

Rabinowitz, D. *No Crueler Tyrannies: Accusation, False Witness, and Other Terrors of our Times (Wall Street Journal Book).* New York: Wall Street Journal Books, 2003.

Reuters (October 23, 2007). Two plead guilty, will testify against O.J. Simpson.

Roberts, O.A. *Outlaws of Cave-in-Rock.* TruTV Crime Library. Schechter, Harold. The Serial Killer Files. New York: Ballantine, 2004.

Rule, A. *The Stranger Beside Me.* New York, NY: Pocket Books: A Division of Simon and Schuster, 2009.

Ryan, Harriet. O.J. Simpson's co-defendants plead guilty, plan to testify against former NFL star. *Court TV* (October 23, 2007).

Sacco, V.F. "Media construction of crime. In (Eds.). G.W. Potter and V.E. Kappeler. *Constructing Crime. Perspectives on Making News and Social Problems.* Long Grove, Il.: Waveland Press (2006), pp. 29-41.

Scaduto, A. *Scapegoat: The Lonesome Death of Bruno Richard Hauptmann.* New York: G.P. Putnam's Sons, 1976.

Schipp, E.R. "O.J. and the Black Media." *Columbia Journalism Review* (1994), p. 39.

Schoolman, J. Gates Still Richest in U.S. Martha Stewart Makes Her Forbes Debut. *New York Daily News*, September, 22, 2000.

Schwartz, A. *The Man Who Could Not Kill Enough.* New York, NY: Birch Lane Books, 1992.

Shover, N. and J.P. Wright. *Crimes of Privilege. Readings on White Collar Crime.* New York: Oxford University Press, 2001.

Smith, A. *The Money Game.* New York; Random House, 1968.

Solomon, E. "Crime sound bites: A view from both sides of the microphone." In (Ed). P. Mason. *Captured by the Media. Prison Discourse in Popular Culture.* Portland, OR: Willan Publishing (2006), pp. 48-64.

Srebnick, A.G. *The Mysterious Death of Mary Rogers: Sex and Culture in Nineteenth-Century New York.* Oxford University Press, Inc., 1995.

Stashower, D. *The Beautiful Cigar Girl: Mary Rogers, Edgar Allan Poe, and the Invention of Murder.* Dutton. Penguin Group (USA), 2006.

Stroman, C.A. and R. Seltzer. "Media use and perceptions of crime." *Journalism Quarterly* (1985), 62: 340-345.

Sullivan, T. and P. Maiken. *Killer Clown*. New York: Grosset and Dunlap, 1983.

Surette, R. *Media, Crime and Criminal Justice. Images, Realities and Policies*. Fourth Edition. Belmont, CA: Wadsworth Publishing, 2007.

Tebbel, J.W. *The Media in America*. Crowell, 1974.

Toobin, J. *End Run at Enron. The New Yorker*, October 27, 2003.

Tuchman, G. *Making News. A Study in the Construction of Reality*. New York: The Free Press, 1978.

Uruburu, P. *American Eve*. Riverhead Books, 2008.

Waller, G. *Kidnap: The Story of the Lindbergh Case*. Dial Press, 1961.

Wally, S., A. Hay and K. Soothhill. "The social construction of rape. *Theory, Culture, & Society* (1983), 2(1): 86-98.

Washington, B.T. *Up From Slavery*. Dover Publications, 1995.

Weitzer, R. Citizens perceptions of police misconduct: Race and neighborhood contexts. *Justice Quarterly* (1999), 16, 816-846.

White, T.H. *The Making of the President 1960*. Harper Perennial, Reissue, 2009.

———. *The Making of the President 1964*. Harper Perennial, Reissue, 2010.

———. *The Fall of Richard Nixon*. Scribner, 1975.

Wolfe, T. *The Bonfire of the Vanities*. Farrar Straus Giroux, 1988.

Woo, E. and E. Malnic. Daryl F. Gates, 1926-2010; Controversial LAPD Chief; Known for key innovation and a combative approach; he saw his leadership challenge as the Rodney King case unfolded. *Los Angeles Times,* April 17, 2010, A1.

Worth, R. *Massacre at Virginia Tech. Disaster and Survival*. Berkeley Heights, NJ: Enslow Publishers, Inc., 2008.

Zorn, R. *Cemetery John: the Undiscovered Mastermind of the Lindbergh Kidnapping.* New York: The Overlook Press, 2012.

ABOUT THE AUTHORS

Dr. Mary Ann Farkas has taught the course, Media and Urban Crime, several times during her twenty years at Marquette University and has incorporated media components in her Corrections, Criminal Court Process, Sex Offenses and Offenders, Women, Crime and Criminal Justice, and Victimology classes. She has written two textbooks for Corrections and Victimology classes: *Correction Leadership: A Cultural Perspective* (Wadsworth/Cengage) with Professor Stan Stojkovic, and *The Dilemma of the Sexual Offender* (Charles C. Thomas Publishing) with forensic psychiatrist Dr. George Palermo. She has also published several book chapters and numerous journal articles.

For over 35 years, Frank Burke has been involved in communications and marketing. His experience has included working with major New York advertising agencies, client firms in both the consumer and industrial sector and, most recently, as a consultant to various companies and institutions. He has written on subjects ranging from technology to politics and frequently appears as guest lecturer on topics including the media and business communication. He has been frequently published in "The American Thinker."

A graduate of the Wharton School of the University of Pennsylvania, Frank was privileged to do undergraduate study at New York University under Professor John Tebbel—a teacher and friend—the author of major studies on the media in America.